Censorship; the C[anadian] Media and Afghanistan: A Historical Comparison with Case Studies

Dr. Robert Bergen

ABSTRACT

Official censorship of the news media by the Canadian government has only occurred twice in the history of the nation: during the First and Second World Wars. Yet, the news media was quick to use the word "censorship" when the first ground rules agreement for the news media was developed by the Canadian Forces during the 1991 Persian Gulf War to restrict what journalists aboard its ships could write about. Canada's involvement in the International Security Assistance Force in Afghanistan provides a rich opportunity to examine whether the Canadian news media faces either official or unofficial censorship in its reporting on the war in Kandahar, the Canadians' area of responsibility. It also provides an opportunity to conduct case study research and to compare and contrast the Canadian news media's coverage of selected Canadian combat operations during the First and Second World Wars, the Korean War, the 1991 Persian Gulf War, the 1999 Kosovo air war and in Afghanistan. This study suggests that journalists and the military alike have both been involved in censorship at different times and to varying degrees throughout these conflicts.

I t will come as no surprise to many that the Canadian Forces (CF) often restricts what the Canadian news media can learn about its military operations in Afghanistan. This paper will demonstrate that the Canadian military is also ready, willing, and able to limit what academics can learn about its restrictions on the news media and what Canadian society as a whole can learn about the Afghan mission. The overarching reality that frames this paper is the truism that freedom of information is not absolute in military affairs but is limited by "operational security" and the varying degrees of commitment on the part of both the Canadian news media and Canadian forces members to keeping Canadians well-informed about Canada's role in the International Security Assistance Force (ISAF) in Afghanistan.

Operational security is "the principle of safeguarding the integrity of a military operation, and/or the safety of the CF members and other personnel involved in the military operation or activity."[1] In Afghanistan, operational security restrictions placed on journalists that limit what they can report upon are enshrined in the ground rules agreement all must sign prior to being "embedded" with the Canadian Forces. Embedding means being able to travel with the Canadian Forces on missions when possible, being provided food and shelter, and given as much access to soldiers as possible given operational security concerns.

A special team of military officers, created in March 2007, adds a second layer of restrictions placed on journalists and others, academics included, severely limiting what Canadians can know about Canada's role in Afghanistan. The so-called "Tiger Team" – the Strategic Joint Staff initiative originally established to scrutinize *Access to Information Act* (ATI) requests related to a number of Military Police Complaint Commission investigations into the handling of Afghan detainees – now has a broad mandate to restrict a wide variety of information about the Afghan conflict.[2] Included in the information that cannot be released is: "Any ATI request for information related to DETAINEES, or Battle Damage Assessments (any report SOP, SIR, sitrep related to IEDs, Vehicle Damage casualties, protection, armour enhancements.)"[3]

Most alarming about this news report is its extensive quoting of a May, 2007, Strategic Joint Staff record documenting the genesis of the team: "This is the first time that the [Canadian Forces] have been engaged in hostilities since the *Access Act* was introduced in 1985. It has been a learning experience and a number of mistakes have been made. We have noted tendencies to be both too restrictive and too open in releasing information."[4]

That statement went unchallenged in the news report. Yet, the first sentence is simply and stunningly inaccurate. The *Access Act* was in place during the 1991 Persian Gulf War and was in use during the 1999 Kosovo Air War. The critical question is: if the author got such historically established facts wrong, what else is inaccurate within the original document? That question offers opportunity to review the history of the restrictions placed on the news media during the 1991 Persian Gulf war to the layers of restrictions it faces in Afghanistan and the strategic implications for the North Atlantic Treaty Organization International Security Assistance Force, (ISAF), to which Canada is but one contributor.

It will shock many academics to learn that the Canadian Forces actively restricted this researcher's attempts to examine the working relationship between the Canadian news media in Afghanistan and the Canadian Forces for this paper. It did that through Canadian Forces Senior Public Affairs

Advisor Lieutenant Commander Al Wong, who instructed this author that there would be no access to the Canadian news media during a research trip by eight Canadian Security and Defence Forum scholars to Afghanistan, which was organized jointly for the first time by the North Atlantic Treaty Organization and the Canadian Department of National Defence from December 12 to December 20, 2007. Wong acted as the group's escort in Brussels, Belgium, and in Afghanistan. The group was technically referred to as stakeholders: "business, academic and community leaders, parliamentarians and others."[5] Its acronym was COLA, short for Canadian Opinion Leaders Afghanistan.

In order to be part of the visiting delegation, on the first leg of the trip at NATO headquarters in Belgium, all members had to sign a stakeholder ground rules agreement and a Code of Service Discipline Acknowledgement for a Visit to a Deployed CF Operation, agreeing to comply with all lawful orders and instructions. These agreements are similar to the documents journalists must sign prior to being embedded with the Canadian Forces in Afghanistan. The major difference between the stakeholders' ground rules and the journalists' ground rules was the absence of the following clause: "Embedded journalists will remain with military escorts at all times and follow their instructions regarding activity and movement."[6]

The restriction on access to the news media was challenged by the author at every turn, including during meetings in Kabul with Canadian Colonel Brett Boudreau, Public Affairs Advisor to NATO's Chairman of the Military Committee and to the Director International Military Staff and with Canadian Ambassador to Afghanistan, Arif Lalani, neither of whom could understand why access to the news media was being denied. No reason was given why access was denied but it is possible to speculate why.

One reason might be that the Forces did not welcome academic scrutiny of its media relations in Afghanistan. Another reason might be that, had the news media learned of the academics' research trip, it could have turned into a news story in Canada. Such a news story might have exposed the Canadian Forces to questions from critics opposed to the mission, which is not to imply that the academics were advocates for it. Thirdly, news of the academics' trip may have conveyed the message to some that the military had created a shadow or alternate panel to the Independent Panel on Canada's Future Role in Afghanistan, chaired by the Honourable John Manley. The academics followed in the footsteps of the panel which had visited Afghanistan the previous week. Regardless, those are political reasons, which have nothing to do with the principle of operational security.

The ground rules are clear: "Ground rules for stakeholders' visit are not intended to restrict the flow of information to non-military visitors. Their purpose is to ensure that classified or operationally sensitive information is not inadvertently released, thereby compromising operational security."[7] One sentence in the ground rules that give on-the-spot discretionary powers to public affairs officers bears examination. "DECPR (Directorate of External Communications and Public Relations) and in-theatre public affairs (PA) staff, in coordination with CEFCOM, *may enhance these ground rules* [my emphasis], as the situation or operation requires." Wide latitude, it would appear, is given to public affairs officers in the exercise of their own judgment.

Regardless, knowing what constitutes an operational security issue and what does not, this author accidentally met a well-known Canadian journalist – Graeme Smith of the *Globe and Mail*, the only correspondent covering Afghanistan full-time – at a dinner hosted by the Canadian Embassy in Kabul. At the first opportunity after dinner, the military's attempt to restrict access to him was discussed with Smith in private and e-mail addresses were exchanged for later correspondence. The Canadian Forces public affairs officer was visibly upset. But, clearly, an academic speaking to a journalist did not assault the integrity of the military mission. He did not jeopardize the safety of the Canadian Forces members and other personnel involved. Had this not been the case, the author would have been removed from the research trip under the terms and conditions of the embedding agreement. The Canadian Forces is a government institution and the literature on State interference in academic freedom is clear and is worth referencing at length:

> It is in this situation that it has become necessary to reassert the medieval ideal of liberties, to argue that Universities have their own independent sphere of judgment, in which the State should not meddle. The argument runs that it is only by this sort of autonomy to govern their own affairs that academics may protect a world in which they are free to exercise their basic rights of freedom of speech and of thought. It is not enough to defend these by the law of the State alone, when the State may, perhaps entirely unwittingly, take away conditions in which these rights can be exercised. The opinion that government is devaluing the standards of the University degree, for example, enjoys only a nugatory freedom if it can only be asserted by spitting in the wind, against opponents who enjoy overwhelming physical and financial power. The standards of the University degree and many other things also, can only ever be defended effectively if they are recognized as purely academic matters, in which the State can have no legitimate say. It is only by defending a medieval liberty, ·

a sphere of academic freedom in which the State does not enter, that academic freedom in a military sense can ever be effectively defended. If the state cannot accept this, Universities should not continue to exist, for they will serve no useful purpose save that of rubber-stamping decisions reached in ignorance by the State.[8]

This is not a paper detailing a government's assault on academic freedom: that is a subject fit for another paper. This topic is mentioned to help the reader understand that the Canadian military's meddling with academic freedom restricted research which most certainly would have widened the scope of this paper on the news media and Afghanistan. There was simply no justifiable operational security reason for that action. Thus, this paper examines the news media's coverage of Canada's involvement in Afghanistan on a continuum that begins with the First World War, and follows with the Second World War, the Korean War, the 1991 Persian Gulf War, and the 1999 Kosovo Air War in order to enable contrasts and comparisons. It is noteworthy that W.H. Kesterton, the pre-eminent authority on the history of Canadian journalism, wrote that the Canadian government has only invoked military censorship twice, during the First and Second World Wars.

The First World War

In Canada, a voluntary press censorship was set up early during the First World War under the Department of Militia and Defence with a Deputy Chief Censor. Canada's communications facilities were meshed with a nationwide cable, radio-telegraph, telegraph, and telephone censorship. That network was tied in with Empire Cable and wireless censorship headed by the Chief Censor in London, England. A September 12, 1914, directive set out information useful to the enemy, dealt with prevention of espionage, security of the Armed Forces, and the welfare of the Canadian people. In June, 1915, regulations made press censorship mandatory, set out what matter was acceptable or unacceptable, and authorized censors who had the power to enter printing and press establishments.[9]

Far removed from the European theatres of war, Canadians were largely informed of the overseas events of the First World War by news reports from the front, which were highly censored by British military authorities. Most of the news reports received were not of the more than 15,600 Canadians dying horribly in less than a month in the mud of Passchendale, but of ridiculously upbeat versions of battle.[10] From the news media's perspective, with the exception of socialist, anti-imperialist, rural and certain French Canadian publications, partisanship was the norm among the nation's major daily newspapers. Typically, the Manitoba *Free Press* proclaimed upon the news that 6,000 Canadians had died at the second battle of Ypres: "above the tears ... there rose steady and clear the voice of thankfulness to God ... that they were permitted in their death to make so splendid a sacrifice."[11]

In lieu of Canadian war correspondents at the front, expatriate William Maxwell Aitken, a successful British newspaperman, became Canada's "Eyewitness" under the authority of the Canadian War Records Office in London. He purposefully made few trips to the front after viewing the horrific second battle at Ypres. He described that battle as an "uplifting and heroic struggle where Canada's superior fighting men sowed the seeds of a proud nationalism."[12] Similarly, he glorified the disaster at St. Eloi's craters in which nearly 1,400 Canadians were accidentally cut down by Allied fire as the result of a lack of communication, difficulties in observation from the rear, and misconceptions of the Canadians' positions. By contrast, 483 Germans were lost. Still, Aitken wrote in his weekly dispatch for the week of April 11 to 18, 1916: "During the period that our troops held in the line in front of St. Eloi the circumstances of the fighting afforded a wealth of opportunity for deeds of daring, and several members of each battalion greatly distinguished themselves in the eyes of their comrades."[13]

Colonel G.W.L. Nicholson, who wrote the official history of the Canadian in the First World War, described St. Eloi as a fiasco and claimed that Aitken knew full well the extent of the disaster. It was Aitken, as the General Representative of Canada at the Front, who cabled Minister of the Militia Colonel Sam Hughes warning him that the British viewed the errors at St. Eloi as serious "and responsibility wide-spreading."[14] That Aitken misled Canadians with his upbeat dispatches about the debacle bothered him not a whit. He explained: "It may not be pleasant to issue false news, but if those at home could be taken into our confidence I feel quite certain they would endorse the scheme."[15] As Humbolt Wolfe wrote, "You cannot hope to bribe or twist, Thank God! The British journalist; But seeing what the man will do, unbribed, there's no occasion to."[16] There was no real need for censorship with Aitken writing such drivel. Most would say that was a dark period in Canadian journalism, but it was little better during the Second World War, as reporting on the Dieppe Raid illustrates.

The Second World War: The Dieppe Raid

Censorship of the news media was set up during the Second World War under the Defence of Canada Regulations that derived their authority from the *War Measures Act* as set out in Chapter 206 of the 1927 Revised Statutes of

Canada.[17] The censors were advisors only and could not prohibit the publication of articles. Newspapers' guilt or non-guilt for violations could only be decided upon by the court. The sole power possessed by the Chief Censor was to say that information was in non-violation, meaning that a newspaper could not be prosecuted if it had obtained censorship clearance. Possible penalties included fines, imprisonment, and suspension.[18]

Against this back-drop, the news coverage of the Dieppe Raid offers a rich case study to illustrate how Canadian journalists who witnessed the carnage on August 19, 1942, reported the news. Nearly 5,000 Canadian soldiers made up the vast majority of 6,000 Allied troops who stormed the heavily defended beach at Dieppe that day in a raid on the German-held French coast. By historical accounts, the action was a tactical disaster that some suggest should never have taken place. Of 4,963 Canadians embarking on their first live action in Europe, only 2,210 returned. Of them, 807 were killed in action, 100 died of wounds, 586 were wounded, and 1,874 were taken prisoner.[19]

Canadian Press war correspondent Ross Munro was among four Canadian journalists who accompanied the Canadian troops as they powered toward the beaches at Dieppe. Munro had covered Canadian training in England and Scotland and was present for Operation Gauntlet, a ten-day Canadian raid in August and September 1941 on the island of Spitzbergen, east of Greenland. Munro was also present for Canadians' training activities for the first planned raid on Dieppe through June and July 1942, although he was unable to report on them for security reasons.[20] The leading histories that address the Dieppe raid's press coverage say that there were two other Canadian correspondents accompanying the troops on the raid.[21] The two most often cited are Fred Griffen of the *Toronto Star* and Wallace Reyburn, London correspondent for the *Montreal Star*.[22] In fact, there was a fourth: radio broadcaster Bob Bowman of the CBC, who used the BBC's facilities to transmit his broadcasts. Army Commander General Andrew McNaughton welcomed the idea of having CBC correspondents along, but accreditation rested with the War Office, which retained a First World War aversion for war correspondents. However, with the help of Canadian High Commissioner Vincent Massey and his assistant, Lester B. Pearson, the CBC received accreditation to the British Expeditionary Force, which gave them access to the entire British-Canadian Front.[23]

All the journalists were in military uniform with war correspondents' badges, but upon arrival in Bath those badges were replaced with second-lieutenants' pips. The exception was the *Toronto Star*'s Griffen a late arrival who was given Canadian army public relations officer Major Cliff Wallace's battle dress. The journalists were clandestinely briefed about the impending Dieppe raid by Wallace in a lattice work summerhouse in the middle of a park.[24] They were told they could report events "honestly and fearlessly within the limitations permitted by considerations of security."[25] Munro, the most experienced war correspondent among them, was assigned to accompany the Royal Regiment that was to land at Puys, while Reyburn was placed with to the South Saskatchewan Regiment that was to land at Pourville. Bowman was assigned to a landing craft carrying the Calgary Tanks. Griffin was in another tank-landing craft carrying the Army Film and Photo Unit that was to land at Dieppe's main beach.

Reyburn's landing craft was the first to reach the beaches at 4:50 a.m. The South Saskatchewans were apparently the only Canadians to take the enemy by surprise. They made it up to the promenade's parapet undetected and began cutting barbed wire before coming under enemy fire. Reyburn made it across the promenade and into a house where a headquarters was established. After leaving that building, he was wounded in the back by shrapnel. The Saskatchewans achieved their objectives by 9 a.m. and had to endure nearly two hours of German fire on the beach before the Royal Navy evacuated them.[26]

Bowman's landing craft, meanwhile, never made it to the beach. It was a sitting duck, bobbing in Dieppe harbour for eight hours as it tried time and time again to land and disgorge its tanks. It was finally driven back by dive-bombers and gunfire, pulling back to the destroyer line and returning to England. While floating offshore, Bowman said he could see German soldiers on the cliffs lobbing grenades on the ships below and knew the engineers and Queen's Own Camerons were getting the worst of the battle.[27]

Munro appears to have witnessed the most bloodshed. As a result, and without disservice intended to the others, this paper focuses on his work. From his vantage point on the landing craft, Munro said he could see sandbagged German positions from the top of the cliff at Puys, in houses and in the cliff's clefts raining machine gun fire down on the hapless Canadians. To his horror, he had to look no farther than his own craft to see its bottom covered with dead troops who had been machine-gunned. The first clue he had that the attack on the main beach had gone horribly wrong was after the boat pulled away from Puys; it attempted to radio the main beach for help with casualties. There was no answer.[28]

From the *Queen Emma*, Munroe could see the Puys beachfront littered with countless Canadian soldiers' bodies, cut down before they could fire a shot. Courageously, he jumped from retreating vessel to retreating vessel in the boat pool in an attempt to ascertain what was happening. At one point, a craft he was in touched down on the main beach, and he made his way across the shale to the sea wall where Canadians lay dead.[29] Later, from an escaping vessel, he watched a furious air battle overhead as landing craft after Allied landing craft were blown out of the water.[30] After the war, he wrote in retrospect that: "On no other front have I witnessed such carnage. It was brutal and terrible and shocked you almost to insensibility to see the piles of dead and feel the hopelessness of the attack at this point."[31]

Some of the first news of the raid on Dieppe appeared in Toronto's *Globe and Mail*, the *Calgary Herald*, and the *Regina Leader Post*, August 19, 1942, the day of the raid. The *Globe* carried a short Canadian Press story on its front page of a communiqué issued by Combined Operations Headquarters, which stated that French citizens had been advised the action was a raid, not an invasion.[32] The *Herald* ran four stories on its front page. Its un-bylined main Canadian Press story from London reported Allied troops were re-embarking from French soil after all chief objectives had been achieved. The source for the story was Combined Operations and Headquarters, which was in the midst of a public relations disaster. While casualties were said to have been heavy, re-embarkation was being conducted as planned. The same story reported that German radio was quickly off the mark and was heard broadcasting that its troops had counter-attacked and repelled the enemy, increasing British losses in men and materiel hourly. It also claimed that Canadian Press correspondent Ross Munro, accompanying the troops, had not been in touch with his office for several days and that his absence paralleled the secret operation. Munro, however, was embroiled in a futile battle with censors.[33] In addition, *Herald* editors ran an analysis, by British United Press War Analyst Louis F. Keemle, on the same page. He wrote that the Dieppe raid set a pattern for the larger invasion to come and that the hour of liberation was not far distant.[34] Keemle had been nowhere near the front. He, nonetheless, said that the striking thing about the action was the perfect co-ordination of the land, sea, and air forces involved. In fact, he wrote, the air force cleared the way by bombing communication lines and centres.[35] That was simply wrong. Air Marshall Arthur Harris refused to allow his heavy bombers to fly after dawn and cancelled the planned heavy air bombardment.

Munro and the other correspondents, meanwhile, made their way to Combined Operations upon their return to England, to file their stories. After Munro's story cleared censors, it ran in hundreds of North American newspapers. While alluding to casualties, saying that half the men on his boat had been wounded; he lauded the Canadians' courage. Under a dateline of August 19 (delayed), he wrote:

> There was heroism at sea and in the skies in those hours, but the hottest spot was ashore, where the Canadians fought at close quarters with the Nazis. They fought to the end, where they had to, and showed courage and daring.

They attacked the Dieppe arsenal of coastal defence. They left
Dieppe silent and afire, its ruins and its dead under a shroud of
smoke.[36]

His work was hailed as a masterpiece and one of the greatest stories of the
war.[37] Elsewhere, Munro's and others' eyewitness accounts were lauded by
the *New York Times* as "rattling good" stories. "It is sensible of the authorities
to let him (the war correspondent) see for himself and to tell what he sees,"
the newspaper said.[38] The problem was, like Max Aitken in the First World
War, Munro made no mention of the Canadians who had been slaughtered. It
could be suggested that he did no more or no less than what countless other
journalists who wrote about Dieppe did, focusing on the positive and not
the negative. The salient difference between Munro and the rest, however,
was that he was the most experienced and knowledgeable of the lot. More
importantly, he was at Dieppe with Canadian soldiers dying all around him.
It was his stories that were reprinted throughout the Allied world. In 1946,
one year after the war ended, Munro admitted he knew at the time that the
raid on Dieppe had turned out much worse than he had written. He wrote:
"I watched those boats in the warm sunshine going back to England empty
when they should have been filled with the thousands of soldiers they'd
taken to France."[39]

What could he have written? Munro accompanied the original training operations for the first July raid that was cancelled due to unfavourable
tides and knew the scope of the original plans, including air bombardment.
He also knew that the new plans were haphazard by comparison.[40] Munro
had also seen plans to blow up a bridge linking Abbeville to Amiens, which
seemed comical to him.[41] He knew what had convinced planners to go ahead
was misleading intelligence that German defences were comparatively thin
and manned by few first-rate troops.[42] He certainly knew the raid had gone
all wrong as far as the detail plan was concerned.[43] Munro wrote nothing
of those things until four years after the raid. In an unapologetic afterword,
he said: "The correspondents who had gone to France with the Canadians
wearily sat down to write their stories. There were many things we could
not tell."[44] Elsewhere, he reiterated that censorship restricted what he could
and could not write, but he argued that most of the time he was able to tell
a story validly despite the censorship. The one exception, he admitted, was
Dieppe. "I never really felt, except maybe on the Dieppe raid, that I was really
cheating the public back home."[45]

The history is clear. The questions raised by the coverage of Dieppe are
why it happened that way and what lessons it may teach about the coverage

of ensuing wars. To say Canada was fighting in an all-out war in which patriotism had to over-ride journalistic integrity does not go far enough. That journalists, even those in war zones decades later, are prone to rely heavily on official military versions of events is well documented.[46] This helps to explain the litany of erroneous propaganda that found its way into Canadian newspapers at the hands of most journalists nowhere near the war zone and by the handful that were.

It has been suggested, again, that, because Munro and the others lived with the Canadian army, went on training courses and manoeuvres, wore uniforms, and were well-known to soldiers and their families, it was unrealistic to expect them to write the truth about what happened at Dieppe.[47] It should be remembered, however, that, before the battle, they were charged by the military to report the events honestly and fearlessly within the limitations permitted by considerations of security. To write the truth about the slaughter would not have been a breach of security because Canadian newspapers eventually carried the truth about the growing numbers of casualties as soon as it became available. Rather, it can be suggested that there were forces at play, that journalistic integrity had been sacrificed on the altar of patriotism.

The Korean War

Like the raid on Dieppe during the Second World War, the Battle of Kap'yong on April 24, 1951, offers a rich case study of some of the news coverage of the Korean War. The major difference between Dieppe and Kap'yong, however, is that where Dieppe was an unmitigated disaster, the battle of Kap'yong on Hill 677 was a stunning victory. The Second Battalion Princess Patricia's Canadian Light Infantry (2PPCLI) held its ground against a massive attack by Chinese soldiers who outnumbered them three to one. The Chinese came at them in waves and were cut down by the Patricia's Bren guns but still kept coming. For their actions, the 2PPCLI were awarded a U.S. Presidential Unit Citation. To this day, it is the only regiment in Canadian history to receive that honour.[48]

The first news of the Chinese assault on nearby Australian positions was reported from Tokyo in Associated Press stories on Tuesday, April 24, which invariably identified the Chinese as "Red troops."[49] One headline, which would likely be considered highly politically incorrect by today's standards, in the *Globe and Mail* that day screamed: "Mongol Hordes Spearhead Drive: Reds Rip Gaping Hole in UN Line, Pour South."[50]

Not until Thursday, April 26, did details of the battle at Kap'yong begin to emerge on Canada's west coast. The *Vancouver Sun* ran an Associated Press story on its front page datelined Tokyo with the headline "Reds Surge toward Seoul." Inserted in the story were three paragraphs in brackets saying: "Bill Boss, Canadian correspondent with the Canadian Battalion, in a dispatch from the west-central sector reported seeing wave after wave of Chinese repelled in a knock-down, drag out battle. Boss said the UN troops, which he could not identify because of security regulations, were in the thick of the Communist onslaught."[51]

The same day, however, other Canadian newspapers carried two variations of a much longer story authored by Boss. The first is worth replicating in its entirety for the astonishing battle details Boss captured. It was headlined in the *Toronto Daily Star*: "Outflanked, encircled Pats won't Quit, Beat Back Reds, Hurl Rifles like spears."[52] It was datelined West Central Sector, Korea, April 26 (CP):

> The Chinese had enough. They withdrew. Throughout Tuesday night and part of Wednesday, the Communist hordes attacked U.N. positions on a steep hill in the west central sector of the flaming Korea Front. They out flanked and encircled these troops who until now had only met with token resistance as they advanced northward.
>
> But, they failed to break a line held by such stalwarts as the sergeant who flung his empty rifle like a spear into the face of the enemy. Or the young company commander who coolly ordered mortar and artillery fire on his own position when his men ran out of ammunition.
>
> (Boss covering the Princess Patricia's in Korea cannot mention "Canadian Troops" or individuals he sees in action because of censorship regulations.)
>
> These troops held steady as rocks as the enemy masses assaulted their hill from the front, from the flanks and finally from the rear where the flanks gave way under sheer weight of numbers. By 6 a.m. yesterday the enemy had had enough. He withdrew down the hill and dug in.
>
> But, he was only 100 yards away screened by a thick curtain of smoke and building up for another attack.
>
> I counted 17 dead Chinese within inches and feet of those troops and approximately 50 graves of enemy buried in the heat of battle. There were uncounted enemy dead where the intended rear and flank attack was thwarted.

It was a hard-won victory. Time and again the Chinese rushed the U.N. front line position and at one time the ammunition of one defending company ran out. And then a young captain, fighting his first action as company commander, ordered his men into slit trenches and called for artillery and mortar fire on the hill.

For three hours, the guns of three field regiments and two battalions of mortars rained down on the position as the captain coolly gave fire directions. It was too much for the Chinese. They moved back.

Wave upon wave, following the orders of whistles and bugles to the split second, the enemy hordes surged in late Tuesday night. It was suicidal, but it evoked this tribute from one sergeant:

"They're good. They were on top of our positions before we knew it. They're quiet as mice with those rubber shoes. There's a whistle. They get up about 10 feet from our positions and come in.

The first wave throws grenades, fires its weapons and goes to the ground. As second does the same, and a third. They just keep coming."

That was the sergeant who hurled his bayoneted rifle like a spear when his ammunition gave out. Another hurled his bayonet at the foes. The sergeant's company held out by dividing the slim remaining supply of ammunition until the enemy pressure ended.

Supplied by Flying Boxcars

The young captain's company was supplied yesterday by "flying boxcars" which made air drops of supplies.

(This portion of Boss's dispatch indicated the company was isolated. Today's eighth Army communiqué reported that an Allied tank battalion broke through and linked up with U.N. forces south of Karangpe.)

Boss said the U.N. forces he was reporting were northeast of Seoul. And he added: "Look at any up-to-date battle map and the thick burr of resistance to the Communist onslaught is in the centre."

(Up-to-date Korean battle maps show that the stiffest fighting is north east of Seoul, near Kap'yong, just south of the 38th parallel which divides North and South Korea. This is almost the centre of the Korean battlefront.)[53]

The same story ran virtually word for word in the *Calgary Herald*, with a shorter version on page 3 of the *Vancouver Sun*. A second version of the same story ran the same day in *The Albertan* and the *Globe and Mail*, although the *Globe*'s byline identified him as William Boss. The only differences in the two versions of the story are the opening five sentences in *The Albertan* and *Globe* stories which read:

> UN mountain warriors won their spurs today, holding their front, refusing to budge though outflanked and encircled.
>
> It was a knock-down, drag-out battle with wave upon wave of Chinese Communists who did everything but drive them from their positions.
>
> These UN troops are on the west central sector north-east of Seoul. Look at any up-to-date battle map and the thick burr of resistance to the Communist onslaught is in the centre.
>
> Cut off and encircled, these UN troops fought on and by late morning today had cleared the enemy from their rear, had beaten them off their flanks and held on their front.[54]

What is interesting about the above stories is that all mention that Boss's report was censored in one way or another. This comment contradicts Kesterton's work that censorship was invoked only during the First and Second World Wars. According to the news reports, censorship regulations prohibited him from reporting that Canadians were involved, let alone specific battalions, individuals, their hometowns, and the operations' or battles' locations. It is also interesting to see how the newspapers got around the censorship. In theatre, Boss could only identify the troops as UN troops, not as the Princess Patricia's. *The Albertan* and the *Globe and Mail*, for example, both ran two sentences above his story saying: "(Bill Boss, Canadian Press correspondent with the Princess Patricia's Canadian Light Infantry in Korea, writes the first detailed report on Wednesday's action. Under censorship regulations, he cannot at the moment, mention Canadian troops, the Patricia's or the home towns of any of the men he interviews.)"[55] Presumably, the censorship was not the full country-wide censorship invoked by the government during the First and Second World Wars, but imposed by the military. While Boss honoured that censorship, the newspapers did not. One cannot envision the government invoking censorship and then having it so flagrantly violated. The *Toronto Daily Star* even went so far as to consult battle maps and correctly identify, in violation of the censorship, Kap'yong, just south of the 38th parallel dividing North and South Korea, as the area where the battle took place. One wonders why the military even bothered to censor locations because it was already clearly apparent that the Chinese troops already knew where the UN troops were when they attacked. In the early 1950s, the idea that such information could be related to the enemy in a timely and strategic fashion is preposterous.

Of the newspapers examined, only the *Halifax Chronicle-Herald* did not use a version of Boss's story, instead running an Associated Press article datelined Tokyo.[56] Presumably the four-hour time difference between Vancouver and Halifax paper's deadlines precluded access to the Boss story.

Particularly striking about Boss's reports is how close he was to the battle. He was able to count dead bodies, witness soldiers calling in mortar fire on their positions, and observe soldiers throwing their rifle and bayonets at the enemy. This is a far cry from Max Aitken's reporting from London during the First World War and is far more in line with the risks the journalists, including Ross Munro, took during the Dieppe Raid during the Second World War. They risked their lives and limbs for their stories, regardless of the final product. Not just anyone would do that.

The 1991 Persian Gulf War

The origins of the ground rules that limit what journalists may write about in Afghanistan can be found in an elaborate communications strategy developed in November, 1990, for journalists travelling on Canadian ships during the Persian Gulf War, the world's first real-time televised war.[57]

In the months leading up to the war, the Canadian Forces viewed the impending conflict as an opportunity to build popular support for the military. Internal military documents obtained using the 1985 *Access to Information Act*, show the military anticipated "maximum disclosure of information consistent with maintaining the operational security of Canada's forces and those of other allied nations participating in the Gulf operations."[58] In its after-action report on its public affairs planning, the Canadian military states that they knew the news media would play an influential role in that communications strategy because the journalists would be the key conveyors of information about, and interpreters of, the war's events to the Canadian public.[59] This report also shows that military public affairs planners made every effort to inform Canadians proactively through a six-pronged communications program.

The first external audience the Forces hoped to target in communication thrusts, via news releases, public briefings, the news media, debates in the House of Commons, and in replies to ministerial questions and inquiries, was the Canadian public. The Forces' second target was the news media, which it planned to stimulate through background briefings, news releases, query responses, and operational theatre visits. The third target audience was elected officials, who would be reached via briefings, questions in the House of Commons, and committee presentations, and through various elected officials' visits to operational theatres. The fourth target audience was Canadian academics, whom the military planned to reach through background and technical briefings. The fifth audience identified was defence analysts who would be reached through technical and background briefings. The sixth audience was ethnic Canadians who would be informed through media reports and public briefings. Finally, the seventh external audience was international publics that would be reached through foreign missions and briefings and assistance to international journalists.[60]

With respect to the news media in particular, the policy was based on operational requirements, as represented by the Forces. It specified:

a. Within the scope of operational security, media will be accorded every possible assistance in the preparation and filing of their reports;

b. Censorship will not be invoked by DND or by CANFORCOMME. The imposition of censorship can only be derived from censorship policy of the Canadian government. Therefore, it is paramount that a good working relationship with the news media be established to ensure they understand the necessity to voluntarily comply with in-theatre security screening guidelines. Accordingly, media covering the roles, operations and activities of the Canadian Forces Middle East should be prepared to submit their copy for security screening only;

c. There will be no suggestion that media expunge critical commentary from their reports unless there is an impact on security of operations;

d. Before they are provided access to in-theatre operations, all media are to be provided unclassified briefings about Canadian Forces operations and activities in the Persian Gulf, security considerations and requirements, and what is expected of them while they are visiting CANFORME units;

e. Media embarked in HMC ships may use ships' communications resources, when appropriate and available. The Canadian Forces will provide protective clothing and equipment to media representatives when they are embarked in HMC ships;

f. All interviews with news media representatives will be 'on the record';

g. Journalists will be requested to dateline their articles and reports generically, such as "... with the Canadian Forces in Bahrain/Qatar/Persian Gulf." No specific locations will be used when filing stories;

h. Media representatives will be assisted by on-site public affairs officers;

j. Diplomatic clearances, visa and inoculations will be the responsibility of the media members; and,

k. Media who are not prepared to work within these guidelines will not be provided access to CANFORME operations, activities and units.[61]

Journalists were required to accept these guidelines in order to be accredited. Despite the military's claim that it wanted to be as transparent as possible, the news media howled over the restrictions placed on them, referring to them as "censorship guidelines." For example, the *Globe and Mail* reported on January 19, 1991, that military censors aboard Canadian ships reviewed journalists' stories to determine whether information in them could jeopardize operational security, while guidelines mirrored U.S. Defense Department guidelines on the prohibition of information that would reveal military operations' details, size, location or movement.[62]

In its lessons-learned analysis of its news-media management, the policy's authors wrestled with the two conflicting imperatives of their practices: openness and candor versus operational security: It recommended: "We should standardize with our allies who have had more operational experience than we have and adopt their more liberal release of info policies."[63]

The 1999 Kosovo Air War

Some eight years after the Persian Gulf Lessons Learned report was written during the 1999 Kosovo Air War, the Canadian Forces ignored its own recommendations to adopt a more liberal release of operational information. University of Leeds scholar Philip M. Taylor predicted, in 1995, that despite rapid advances in communications technologies, militaries had two means to effectively censor the modern news media during a conflict. First, access to troops could be denied altogether and, second, military leaders could control messages about the conflicts by inserting themselves into the news-gathering process.[64] Air wars, particularly, lend themselves to such censorship quite nicely because it is impossible for journalists to accompany pilots on combat missions. As a result, crews can only be interviewed before or after their missions and cockpit footage of bombs being released might possibly be obtained.[65] Taylor predicted, however, that what such images could not convey were the "sounds, sight, smell, touch, and taste of the nasty, brutal business of people killing people" which would frighten, appall, and repel most people. "That reality of war evades media war."[66]

During the Kosovo Air War, both censorship techniques were used. News media who travelled Aviano, Italy, to report on the Canadian air force participation in the North Atlantic Treaty Organization's seventy-eight-day bombing campaign, were not permitted on the American air base. Completely denied access to the Canadian crews, the news media members had to rely on the goodwill of the Task Force Aviano commander, Colonel Dwight Davies, which was in short supply.[67] Davies had no time for the news media whom he thought belittled the efforts of his air crews, questioning their proficiency at hitting targets.[68] He also believed, wrongly, that Canadian pilots identified in news reports during the 1991 Gulf War had body bags thrown on their families' lawns by protestors opposed to the war. As a result, he would not let the few pilots who eventually did speak to reporters identify themselves or discuss details of their missions.

The Canadian Forces staged daily news briefings on the progress of the war, but they contained very little specific information about operations and no accounts of missions' successes or failures. During one briefing, the most high-profile interview of the campaign, journalists in Ottawa talked to one unidentified Canadian CF-18 pilot in Aviano via a telephone conference call about his feelings about flying into combat for the first time, but little else.[69] Effectively, all life was stripped out of the journalists' few reports from Aviano, print or television. In Ottawa, "operational security" was invoked time and again as a reason for not releasing information, ludicrously at times. The June 1, 1999, briefing was indicative of how "operational security" came into play. One journalist tried to get a sense of what the Canadians were doing in the bombing campaign by learning about the number of bombs dropped. He was stonewalled by Chief of Joint Operations Brigadier General David

Jurkowski on the grounds of security. The reporter wanted to know the cost of the weapons dropped to date, and Jurkowski replied: "That could lead one to think about the number of weapons and by way of policy and security, we don't talk about the number of weapons employed."[70] The journalist pressed further, wanting to know why the number of bombs was a security issue and arguing that Canadians had a right to know the cash value of munitions dropped. Jurkowski replied: "I have those numbers for you right now and for security reasons, I'm not going to address it any further."[71]

This line of questioning was dropped until the next day when Deputy Chief of Defence Staff Lieutenant General Ray Henault was asked about the cost of bombs. Henault went on the offensive telling the journalists: "We have been, I think, fairly open. In fact, very open throughout this whole process now at seventy-one days of giving you briefings daily so I think our process has been very open and transparent, probably in a way unprecedented in the past."[72] Henault then contradicted Jurkowski's previous argument by divulging that $20 million had been spent on Operation Echo, of which 45 per cent was on bombs.[73] The journalists did not question the inconsistency in security considerations – why precise information was withheld for security reasons one day, and was not a security issue the next.

In the end, a content analysis of the entire daily news media coverage in Canada of the seventy-eight-day war including both print and television, revealed that nearly 60 per cent had two sentences or less about the CF-18s' involvement. Slightly more than 75 per cent had six sentences or less. Not much can be learned about a war in six sentences or less.[74]

Documents obtained under the *Access to Information Act* reveal that the Canadian Forces' lessons-learned report of the news media coverage of the Kosovo Air War did not analyze the success or failure of the Canadian Forces public affairs policy and practices, as had the lessons-learned report on the 1991 Gulf War. Rather, that campaign was assessed specifically to illustrate the ethical dilemmas it presented for the media and public's right to know versus operational security and care of personnel. The language is cryptic in that it avoids specifics and, in the end, paints a self-serving picture of its public-affairs practices.[75] It reads:

> The subject of military security vs embarrassing information vs the public right to know will become a routine dilemma in future operations. The Kosovo campaign example of providing constant media briefings and the strategy reflecting candor, truth and disclosure to the extent possible would appear to represent a strategy that fulfills our obligations of public disclosure and should serve to build public trust and confidence. Decisions to

fully and promptly report any incident similar to the Chinese embassy bombing in Serbia are seen as consistent with defence ethical values. The questions of 'What to report?' will always require a balancing of values, security issues and the ethic of care (morale) of our people.[76]

While the report claimed that daily briefings were a model for public disclosure, balancing operational security concerns with the public's right to know, in reality, there was no balance at all. The 1991 recommendation that Canada adopt the more liberal release of information policies of their more operationally experienced allies was ignored. Worse, the "operational security" reason which the Forces used to undermine any democratic role for the news media during the 1999 air war was based on myth. Many air force commanders believed that the families of Canadian airmen during the 1991 Gulf war, identified in news media reports, had body bags dumped on their lawns in a bid to intimidate those serving overseas. That never happened. A myth should not have driven operational security concerns that undermined the democratic role of the news media during war, but it did. And, as a result of it, the Canadian public knows nothing about Canada's involvement in the Kosovo Air War. It is an information black hole. Canadians deserve much better.

Kabul, Afghanistan

Canadians have been deploying to Afghanistan since February 2002. It was abundantly clear very early on from the Canada military's own analyses of the news media's coverage of the Afghanistan conflict that the Canadian Forces study the news media, learn lessons about it – even if at times the lessons are ignored – and write about it in a scholarly fashion in refereed journals. This accumulated body of wisdom is thus diffused throughout the command chain of the Forces in order to better manage the media. They work from a 123-page *Public Affairs Handbook*, first developed on January 15, 1974, amended in September 1985, and amended again in March 1999, specifically intended to control all manner of messages and images that could affect how the Forces appear publicly, including in the news media.[77] There is no equivalent document in Canadian newsrooms or journalism schools. The most comprehensive guide that journalists have which deals with the Canadian Forces is comprised of five pages in *The Canadian Press Stylebook*. It sets out the proper way to refer to the Forces, where headquarters are, the proper way to use titles and ranks before a name, how to refer to retired officers, that courts martial are open to the media, a section on ceremonies and miscellaneous information which includes the tidbit that Canadians do not go to boot camp, they take basic training.[78]

The military's scholarly approach to the news media is no more evident than in a Fall/Winter 2004 article in the *Canadian Army Journal* by Major Jay Janzen, which examines the nature of the relationship between the news media and the military from Rotation Zero (ROTO 0) of Operation Athena in the summer of 2003 when Canadian journalists were embedded with the 3 Royal Canadian Regiment (RCR) Battalion Group based out of Kabul, Afghanistan.

That relationship was based on a ground rules agreement, founded on the American experience in Iraq, established to manage the journalists who would be hosted by the 3 RCR.[79] The Canadian military learned that there were big differences between the American concept of embedding in Iraq and the Canadians' Afghanistan experience. In the Iraq war, for example, individual journalists were assigned to specific units for the duration; eating, sleeping, and travelling with the same unit for months, receiving briefings from platoon or company commanders with scant public affairs experience.[80] As a result, they had little contact with public affairs officers or senior commanders who lost their ability to influence the journalists from a strategic perspective.[81]

The Canadian journalists, meanwhile, were based at Camp Julian in separate living quarters from the troops. There were eight journalists from five different media organizations in regular contact with public affairs and senior officers. The latter learned, as an effective media relations tactic, that by being proactive with journalists, they could influence what they covered. Major Janzen explained:

> On many occasions, senior officers would join members of the media for meals or a cup of coffee. These impromptu gatherings suggested to journalists that they were not regarded as an inconvenience or something to be avoided. Further, it gave both parties an opportunity to hold informal discussions that would often lead to positive story ideas being passed to journalists. Many company commanders also sought out journalists when their troops were about to embark on interesting or important missions. Reporters appreciated being given information on upcoming activities rather than having to discover it on their own. By pushing information to the media, the battalion was also able to exercise some influence over what journalists decided to cover.

When an opportunity to cover a mission or event was proactively presented to a reporter, it almost always received coverage.[82]

Major Janzen wrote that it was preferable, from the military's point of view, to have journalists remain in theatre for extended period because interactions with them tended to be more cordial than with those who remained for only short periods of time, or who chose not to be embedded. Non-embedded journalists, who did not sign the embedding agreement, often called "unilateral" journalists, sometimes just came and went or lived off camp. Anywhere off camp is routinely referred to as "outside the wire." It was better to have embedded journalists with Canadian troops rather than unilaterals. Senior officers personally welcomed the embedded journalists, and pro-actively pursued professional relations with them, ensuring a high-level of support by informing them of potential story opportunities. The benefit, it was said, was that the media were properly informed. In the end, clear preference was given to journalists who embedded for extended periods of time.[83]

Even then, it was not possible to accommodate all the journalists who wanted to be embedded within rifle companies on operations because there were only three such units. The solution was to develop a rotating schedule, which did not facilitate the building of solid relationships between soldiers and journalists. A similar problem emerged with allowing journalists to cover operations in such small vehicle patrols as the Iltis because three of its four seats had to go to military members. Some journalists from larger organizations even rented their own vehicles to accompany the soldiers when possible.[84]

The single biggest problem, documented by Major Janzen, was disputes over access the media had to information that the Forces deemed forbidden to them for reasons of operational security. Janzen notes the news media members were routinely briefed on impending operations and were provided sensitive material to help them understand and report to Canadians about the overall mission being conducted by the Canadian military in Kabul, but were not allowed to report on them until authorized by unit commanders. During ROTO 0 of Op ATHENA, members of the media had a moderate level of access to operational information. However, they were uncertain as to whether they could even mention simple information such as the name of a vehicle or an approximation of how many soldiers were in the 3 RCR Battalion Group. Many of these concerns were alleviated by when public affairs staff at National Defence Headquarters in Ottawa produced theatre-specific ground rules in November 2003, based on the 1991 media policies, as well as comprehensive briefings to better define the boundaries between releasable and non-releasable information.

Embedded journalists were required to sign the ground rules agreement, which was far more restrictive than that for the 1991 Persian Gulf War, which the news media of the day claimed was censorship. While this agreement did not require the media covering the roles, operations, and activities of the Canadian Forces in Afghanistan to submit their copy for security screening, unlike the 1991 agreement, it did provide nineteen categories of information that could not be released unless specifically approved by the Task Force Commander and ten categories that could. Among the eminently reasonable information that could not be reported was "specific information on troop strength, equipment or critical supplies (e.g., artillery, radars, trucks water, etc.)" and "information on future operations, current operations, postponed or cancelled operations" and the like.[85] Among those that could be reported were the "arrival of military units in the area when officially announced," and "non-sensitive, unclassified information regarding air and ground operations, past and present" and, lastly, the laughable "weather and climate conditions" category.[86] No responsible journalist would report on future operations. The public's right to know is not worth risking the life of even one soldier. But, the ground rules set out in 2003 trivialized the work of serious journalists risking their lives in Afghanistan, when the Canadian Forces operational-security-minded brain trust in Ottawa cleared them to report on the weather. (See Appendix One for a complete list of the releasable and non-releasable information developed for use in 2003.)

Without being specific, Major Janzen wrote that journalists were generally trustworthy regarding operational security when the rationale for restricting certain information was explained to them. But, many became impatient when, for example, there were rocket attacks against Camp Julien where they were based. They would leave their assigned protected areas seeking imagery, sounds, and impressions of the event, eventually forcing them to be placed under the escort of a public affairs officer. Further, the journalists were not told about highly sensitive operations such as the potential arrest of terrorists or contingency plans for the Afghan government's defence, because the potential for security breaches was extreme.[87] The problem with that approach, Janzen noted, was that Canadians reading or watching the news at home "can be left with impression the Canadian Forces are involved in a soft peacekeeping mission, when in fact troops are being deployed on some dangerous and sensitive missions."[88] The challenge, he wrote, was to strike a balance so the media could report on aspects of the missions while maintaining elevated levels of operational security. In the end, Janzen concluded that, overall, with only a few periods of tension, the embedding program was successful, thanks to an "outstanding commitment of the chain of command at all levels to support journalists in their efforts to cover the operation."[89]

Canadian journalists simply do not access the Canadian Forces in the scholarly fashion that the military studies them. There are no peer-reviewed journals to which they contribute reflections on their success or failure as an industry to cover the 1991 Persian Gulf War or the 1999 Kosovo Air War. Having said that, despite Major Janzen's upbeat assessment of the embedding program in the *Canadian Army Journal*, the Canadian Press's Stephen Thorne, a member of the Canadian War Correspondents Association (C.W.C.A.), said the wheels were falling off the embedding program while he was in Kabul between 2003 and 2004. He claimed, in the Fall 2004 C.W.C.A. newsletter, then Lieutenant General Rick Hillier, who commanded the International Security Assistance Force between February and August, 2004, and Brigadier General Jocelyn Lacroix, who was commander of the Kabul Multi-National Brigade, denied media access to Canadian Forces operating with Afghans when they apprehended terrorists believed responsible for a mine strike that killed two Canadians in October 2003, in addition to seizing weapons caches and explosives. Instead, Thorne claimed the generals wanted the journalists to cover "routine patrols, goodwill projects and base politics" which grossly misrepresented Canadians' Afghan role.[90] Thorne explained that operational security had no bearing on Hillier's reticence in that regard:

> In a meeting soon after I arrived in Kabul last March, Hillier told me his concerns had "nothing to do with operational security." He said the decision was a political one, based partly on the sensitivities of other NATO participants and on the fact the ISAF leadership didn't like the way the earlier raids had been covered. Canadian troops got way too much credit for the arrests and seizures at several area compounds last spring, Hillier said. He said one of the aims of such operations was to put Afghan police and national security forces at the forefront of operations. He said the credibility and legitimacy of ISAF and the Afghan government depended on the appearance that Afghan forces were capable of handling their own affairs – even if ISAF backup was required.[91]

According to Thorne, about a month later, General Hillier recanted his political argument, claiming his concern over the news media coverage was based on operational security. He wrote:

The Vandoos' leadership actually believed that Canadian newspaper coverage of a raid involving the Royal Canadian Regiment in January was responsible for a suicide bombing. Other soldiers told me this could not have been true – that it was evident that the bombing had been very carefully planned and it would have been impossible for anyone to have organized it so quickly; they also said it was evident it was an attack on ISAF, not on the Canadians specifically. Not to mention the fact that spies – and cell phones – are everywhere in Afghanistan and news travels faster than any news service could ever hope.[92]

As a result, Thorne wrote, although the news media were ostensibly to have privileged access to the troops and their operations as result of the media embedding program, in reality, the embeds were "often the last to hear about anything that happened at brigade or ISAF headquarters."[93] While Thorne is critical of Hillier, Lacroix, and Captain Bernard Dionne, a public affairs officer, the most valuable contribution his piece makes is to show a marked difference in various soldiers' attitudes and commitment toward preserving one of the most basic democratic values – a free press. In that regard, he singled out Major Janzen, Major Luc Gaudet, Captain Richard Langlois, Captain Mike Mailloux, and Lieutenant Colonel Roland Lavoix as "pillars of co-operation, hard work and professionalism who appeared to respect the embedding program, were committed to it and understood the job that the media were there to do."[94]

In March 2006, the *Toronto Star*'s Mitch Potter broke new ground in the media's coverage of conflict through the detail he provided of a horrific axe attack on Lt. Trevor Greene, who was part of a Canadian Forces Civil-Military Co-operation (CIMIC) platoon visiting a destitute Afghan village, which the *Star* could not identify for security reasons.[95] As part of CIMIC's outreach, Greene – a Vancouver reservist attached to the Princess Patricia's Canadian Light Infantry's First Platoon of Alpha Company – had removed his helmet, laid down his weapon, and sat on the ground with village elders in a March 4 "shura" or meeting, in an attempt to build bridges and determine their needs. Out of nowhere, a young man, less than twenty years old, brandishing a hidden axe, swung it into the top of Green's head. Potter was embedded with the platoon. Although he was elsewhere in the village and did not witness the attack, he nevertheless was able to directly interview platoon members, including Commander Captain Keven Schamuhn who sat next to Greene in the meeting and who saw the attack take place. The following is part of his exclusive report in the Sunday *Star* on March 5:

"I began the conversation with an introduction and turned things over to Trevor (Greene). He was asking about whether the village had a school when the attack came."

Schamuhn said he caught a peripheral glimpse of the attacker raising his arm, but was unable to see what was in his hands. A moment later, he watched in horror as the man shouted "Allahu Akbar" (God is great) and swung the axe down on Greene.

"I could see the poison in his eyes," Schamuhn said of the attacker. "His eyes were bulging out. And after he swung the axe, he stood there frozen. He knew what was about to happen."

Schamuhn and two other Canadian soldiers standing metres away reached for their weapons.

Sgt. Rob Dolson, a nine-year veteran of Alpha Company, was first to respond, firing into the assailant, who stumbled but did not fall. Schamuhn and Pte. Matt McFadden followed up with bursts from their C8 semi-automatic assault rifles.

The attacker dropped to the ground, his body rolling down the slope toward the river.[96]

Altogether, the three soldiers fired fourteen rounds into the attacker.[97] The embedding agreement in place at the time placed no control over the reports of incidents eye-witnessed by reporters. But, when other embedded journalists at Kandahar Air Field (KAF) learned of the attack on Greene, they also wanted an opportunity to interview the soldiers. Canadian Forces public affairs officers subsequently arranged a teleconference call with Captain Schamuhn who provided a highly emotional and detailed account of the attack, including the names of the soldiers who killed the assailant and how many shots were fired. That was too much information for the public affairs advisors, who embargoed the details on the grounds that they put those soldiers at risk or violated individual privacy. As a result of the embargo, which the public affairs officers could invoke under the embedding agreement, the nasty, brutal business of Canadian soldiers killing an enemy evaded Canadians in reports filed by all the journalists except for the *Star*'s Potter and Canadian Press's Les Perreaux. Perreaux in the *Chronicle-Herald* and the *Winnipeg Free Press* identified Schamuhn as one of three soldiers who fired at the assailant, killing him instantly. This was at odds with the *Star*'s report that it took two bursts, from Captain Schaumhn and Private McFadden, to kill Greene's assailant.[98]

Canadian public affairs officer Captain (N) Chris Henderson explained his thinking about the way the media was managed in the Greene attack in the Spring 2006 edition of the *Canadian Military Journal*. Henderson also offered his thoughts on amendments to the media embedding guidelines so to further restrict journalists when Canadian Forces killed the enemy in the future, once again illustrating the military's highly sophisticated scholarly approach to managing the news media.

> The March 4 axe attack on Captain Trevor Greene brought two such amendments into focus. As described above, the attacker in that incident was shot dead by Canadian Forces personnel. Following a request from media embedded at Kandahar Air Field, and thus physically removed from the soldiers involved, a teleconference call was conducted with the platoon commander, Captain Kevin Schamuhn. The interview was evocative, emotional and highly detailed, including the names of the soldiers who killed the assailant, the number of shots they fired, as well as a description of Capt. Greene and his vital signs following the attack. This resulted in a decision to embargo certain elements of the interview as they were deemed to put the involved soldiers at risk or to violate the privacy of an individual. This suggests an amendment to the embedding rules that would preclude the naming of soldiers involved in actions resulting in the death of enemy fighters and insurgents or friendly forces and/or the specific details of such an action that are precluded by the rest of the media embedding guidelines. Further analysis is needed to resolve this question if soldiers themselves wish to speak with the media.
>
> This incident also underscored the necessity to insulate soldiers involved in combat operations from media contact in the immediate aftermath of that action. While there is no standard or recommended period of exclusion from a mental health perspective, media contact should be avoided at least until affected soldiers receive critical incident stress debriefing – should the chain of command deem such a debriefing necessary. If there is no critical incident stress debriefing, the chain of command must make an assessment of the soldiers' capacity to conduct media interviews while remaining within the bounds of operational security and propriety. Public affairs officers must be available to

provide their advice to the chain of command, and assist in pre-paring interview subjects if appropriate. This additional rigour is not intended to override the extant CF policy governing pub-lic affairs, DAOD 2008. However, in situations involving death or injury, additional steps appear necessary to protect both the soldiers and operational security.[99]

Henderson's article refers to Mitch Potter's article in the *Toronto Star*, which named Captain Schamuhn, Sergeant Dolson, and Private McFadden, along with the number of shots fired and when. Whether their identification in a newspaper half a world away would violate operational security and put them at greater risk from largely illiterate enemies who do not speak English is debatable. Privacy, however, could be an issue. It is reasonable to sug-gest that the soldiers who killed Greene's assailant should be unidentified for privacy considerations. But to embargo the number of shots fired and how in that instance or any other in the interest of "operational security" is not reasonable. Its only effect is to rob Canadians of any insight into how professionally their soldiers performed in horrific wartime circumstances. Canadians deserve to know that. Canadians need to know, not only how Canadian soldiers are killed, but how well they are trained and how well they perform. The details are grim, but if Canadians can stomach seeing pictures of blood-drenched corpses and victims being hauled out of build-ings in Mumbai following the November 26, 2008, terrorist attack, they can stomach the thought of Canadian soldiers killing and being killed. The line could be drawn at pictures of Canadian bodies, but otherwise they see worse in movies. Our soldiers are fighting a war in Afghanistan. Canadians need to understand that and eyes are so much more open than minds.

The other point that must be made in a scholarly fashion about Captain Henderson's article in the *Canadian Military Journal* is that journalists do not address such important matters that have a direct bearing on their work. That difference is what makes soldiering a profession and journalism a craft – a craft of a higher calling, it should be said, but a craft nonetheless. It will be shown in due course how the Canadian Forces responded to the recom-mendations in Henderson's article.

A number of prominent Canadian journalists have criticized the media embedding program as it existed in their tenure, which merits examination of their experiences in Afghanistan. Rosie DiManno and Mitch Potter, of the *Toronto Star*, questioned in April 2006 whether journalists could be fully independent while embedded with the Canadian Forces, but lamented that they had little choice due to the dangers in Kandahar:

Canadian soldiers are there in a new and difficult hybrid role – sometime combatants, sometime diplomats. Journalists want Canadians to know whether the strategy is working and at what cost. The military wants its story told as well. What are the options for journalists who want to do that? In Kandahar, escalating dangers so limit Western journalists' movements that the risks can outweigh the benefits of being there as an independent observer. The military offers access, security, information, technical backup and arguably the only chance right now to cover the Canadian Forces there.[100]

That reality, coupled with the fact that the Canadian Forces does not want information published on current operations, weighed heavily upon David Walmsley, the *Star*'s assistant managing editor for national and foreign news, but he was able to rationalize holding off on the reporting of breaking news so long as the fact was explained to the newspaper's readers.

The military does not want published information to jeopardize a current operation. Reporters may be aware of military plans and might even accompany troops, but the story will not be told until the operation is over. "The issue is more timing than censorship," Walmsley said, adding that the short-term disadvantage of a delay in informing readers is worth the longer-term benefit of giving readers the additional information and detail possible because a reporter was there. And so the line between giving and withholding information is paced constantly. In fairness to the readers, it is also essential that every story written by an embedded reporter include a line that explains this is so – a practice which has been unevenly applied.[101]

DiManno was quoted in the article as saying she would much rather be a unilateral than an embedded reporter and thought the best solution, as did Potter, was to have two reporters on the ground: one embedded and one unilateral so to report all dimensions. The *Globe and Mail*'s Christie Blatchford also wrote about embedding in 2006 and took a tongue-in-cheek swipe at Lawrence Martin, a *Globe* colleague, who questioned embedded journalists' ability to deliver the news with a "50–50" balance of objectivity. She argued there is no difference between embedded journalists holding back information and Ottawa's Parliamentary journalists embargoed from reporting budget details on budget day. She wrote:

> Dear God, you want to talk about embedding, honey? Now, Laurie is more of an independent crank than most but Ottawa-centric reporting, where journalists, bureaucrats, mandarins, lobbyists and MPs share small and oft-overlapping social circles – not to mention the guiding belief that a fart from one of their own is inherently more interesting and important than, oh, a flood in the dreary Prairies – is a more insidious form of embedding than what my colleagues and I were doing in Afghanistan....
>
> Now, there is some terrific reporting that comes out of the nation's capital (this is my version of Mr. Martin's patronizing bone to the effect that some embedded reporters do, you know, good work) but a much bigger whack of it is press-release, press-conference, media-staged, event-driven hooey....
>
> At least reporters embedded with the military sign off on the deal. We know what we are for the duration of our stint, and so does the military: It's a straight-up arrangement. In exchange for gaining unusual access to the troops, we agree not to publish certain kinds of information (precise numbers of soldiers on the ground, pictures of military installations), we agree to certain kinds of temporary embargoes (we get briefed in advance on particular missions, for instance, but sometimes have to wait until the soldiers get safely in place before publishing – gee, just like budget day in Ottawa!) and to abide by the military's rules.[102]

Blatchford also addressed a new phenomenon in Afghanistan: the phenomenon of "fixers" reporting the news. Fixers in journalism are not new. These are local residents hired to help as drivers and translators and for their knowledge and contacts. Some fixers in Afghanistan have contacts in the government of Hamid Karzai, others with warlords and the Taliban. A good fixer in Afghanistan can command up to $1,500 a month, a fortune in a country where the average annual income in 2006 was $250.[103]

The new phenomenon taking place in Afghanistan and Iraq to which Blatchford referred, however, is the practice of fixers going alone to places where it is far too dangerous for Western reporters to venture and, in effect, becoming the reporter/photographer/cameraperson. She said: "This in itself is weird and unsettling journalism because in practice what it sometimes means in places such as Afghanistan and Iraq is that fixers go places with their cameras that are too dangerous for Western reporters, with the result that we then rely on the fixers' eyes and ears, not to mention their common fetish for close-ups of the dead, and not on our own."[104]

This important issue raises ethical questions. Without a Western reporter, it is not possible to say with certainty whom the fixers' sources are. Are they family or friends? How representative are such sources? Are the fixers' ethics on par with those of Canadian journalists? Could the information have been gathered any other way? On the other hand, Afghanistan remains one of the most dangerous places in the world for a journalist to work independently; should new rules apply for fixers just as new rules do for embedded journalists?

A footnote to Ms. Blatchford's April 8 thoughts on the embedding program is that she did not discuss an incident that happened to her on April 2, when she, photographer Louie Palu, *Toronto Star* columnist Dimanno, and Ontario-based freelance filmmaker Richard Fitoussi were removed from accompanying Canadian Forces after complaints from allies. The four were attached to the Princess Patricia's Light Infantry battle group, which was operating with the U.S. Special Forces, who complained about their presence. The Canadian Press obtained information about the incident nearly eight months later, in December, using the *Access to Information Act.* In a subsequent story, Canadian Press's Jeff Esau wrote that filmmaker Fitoussi said that, at the time, they were told they were being evacuated for their own safety. In reality, unidentified allies had complained about their presence. Esau talked to military officials in Ottawa who told him that "placating Canada's allies will always take precedence over the embedding program. 'Our allies having full confidence in working with Canadians in all operations trumps embeds being on those operations.'"[105] There is little doubt the journalists would have written about their removal had they known it was not for their own safety – and they do have to trust the Forces on safety issues. But there is also little doubt the Forces will mislead journalists if it suits its purpose.

Meanwhile, Blatchford's *Globe* colleague, Geoffrey York, spent four weeks embedded with the Canadian Forces in Afghanistan in May of 2006. He approached the assignment with a healthly dose of skepticism. York is an elder statesman of conflict reporting, with more that fifteen years of experience covering conflicts such as the Russians in Chechnya, the Americans in Iraq, and the Canadians in Somalia. He was also one of the journalists completely shut out of the Canadian operations in Aviano, Italy, during the Kosovo Air War in 1999. He always prefers to work as independently as possible as a so-called unilateral because he thinks that the military tends to be a small part of a greater story of human tragedy and national anguish. He wrote:

The embedding experience had appeared, to me, to be a narrow and restricted way to approach a war zone. So I was skeptical about my assignment in Kandahar last month. Four weeks embedded on a military base? Was it the right way to cover Canada's role in Afghanistan?

The Globe's editors had wrestled with the same questions, of course, and ultimately we decided that we needed to be embedded to stay close to Canada's troops. But for me, it was also a personal quandary. After seeing the benefits of independence in every other war zone, could I handle the restrictions and censorship of embedded life?[106]

It did not take long for York to run straight into the wall of operational security. Within a just a few days, he discovered the power handed over to military public affairs officers as a result of him signing the embedding agreement. He explained:

It was long after nightfall at the Kandahar Air Field, and I had already told my editor about the article that I planned to write. Then the Canadian military spokesman marched into my tent with a curt announcement: He was killing the story.

He acknowledged that the story was accurate and truthful and that another Canadian spokesman had already confirmed the facts of it. But he uttered two magic words – "operational security" – and announced that the media were not permitted to publish the story. It had to die.

And what was that story I was forced to kill? A report that Canadian troops had shifted away from a forward operating base – something that must have already been obvious to any resistance fighters paying any attention to the place. And even if they weren't, it's hard to imagine that the Taliban would pick up military secrets from the pages of a Canadian newspaper.[107]

York wrote that he ended up with mixed feelings about his embedding experience in Kandahar and that the assignment was more complicated than he anticipated. And, like the Canadian Press's Stephen Thorne before him, the amount of discretionary power wielded by public affairs officers and their commanders varied widely from soldier to soldier.

Yes, there was censorship – sometimes for reasons that seemed inexplicable. Yes, there were heavy-handed attempts to control the story, to suppress photos, to spin messages and to deny reality. But there was something endearingly Canadian about it all. Our spin doctors just couldn't manage the ruthlessness of a Pentagon media campaign.

Despite all the stonewalling instincts of their Ottawa masters, the Canadian soldiers were unable to suppress their own sincerity and honesty – their genuine belief that they were doing good work for humanity and the media should be allowed the freedom to see it.

I felt a little sorry for the hard-working military spokesmen – decent guys like Major Mario Couture and Major Marc Theriault – who were caught between the conflicting demands of the pushy journalists and the evasive military commanders. They struggled to persuade their bosses to make statements to the press, but they were fighting an entrenched bureaucracy, infected with Ottawa's penchant for secrecy and timidity.

The great advantage of embedding is the chance to see Canada's soldiers at work, and the chance to help our readers understand the future of their military – a new mandate that combines the traditional warrior role and an emerging humanitarian role. Canada's rank-and-file soldiers are mostly a highly impressive group: courageous and professional, articulate and thoughtful, and genuinely believing in the complex task of fighting extremists while helping an impoverished society.

Yet embedding is a double-edged sword. Propaganda is always central to the tactics of any army, and the Canadian military certainly tries to exploit the media.

It's difficult for an embedded journalist to penetrate the wall of secrecy that surrounds the military coalition. We still do not know, for example, which troops ordered the air strikes that killed at least 17 civilians in a village near Kandahar last week – we do not even know the nationality of those troops. So there is no accountability for the killing of those villagers.[108]

Certainly, the Canadians could claim that without Canadian warplanes in Afghanistan, Canadians could not have bombed the villagers. But, York makes a subtle distinction in his reporting of that incident in which civilians were accidentally killed. He says we still do not know which troops "ordered" the air strikes, and then Canadians do have the power to call in close air support from American or French warplanes. As for the restrictions imposed by the embedding agreement, a partial solution which the *Globe* employs is having its reporters in Kandahar make a habit of getting into the local communities in search of a more balanced perspective.

By the late summer and fall of 2006, senior federal officials became alarmed about the mostly negative news coming out of Afghanistan, particularly in light of fifteen Canadian soldiers who had been killed in just seven weeks. E-mail files obtained by the *Globe and Mail* from that period revealed that the Canadian public affairs officers in Afghanistan began aggressively selling or "pushing" development and reconstruction stories to journalists embedded with the Forces in Afghanistan. It showed the military public affairs officers successfully changed the direction of the news coverage. The *Globe* wrote:

> "Obviously, the major concern at [at PCO] is whether we are pushing development and [Foreign Affairs Canada] issues with embeds," Maj. (Norbert) Cyr told his military colleagues.
>
> The Canadian Forces, in an e-mail reply to the Privy Council Office, rejected the notion that it wasn't doing enough to focus on development work conducted by other departments across government.
>
> "This cannot be further from the truth.... The daily effort in theatre and domestically is to demonstrate the overall contribution of Canada," wrote Sue Daly, a public affairs manager.
>
> "There is an appetite to have more stories to pitch and [we] would be happy to facilitate this if there is anything you are looking at profiling."
>
> In the same e-mail, the military provided the Privy Council Office with a list of upcoming coverage plans among the embedded media, including the Canadian Press and *Journal de Quebec*, as well as the location of various journalists accompanying soldiers in Afghanistan.
>
> "I think you will see from the movements of the embeds below and the coming plans for interviews that the [public affairs officers] have been quite successful in their efforts to get the embeds to focus their attention elsewhere than the military kinetic [combat] operations," Ms. Daly wrote.[109]

The embedding agreement is but one way that the military controls the news media in Afghanistan. There is a second element that, again, speaks volumes about the Canadian Forces – from the generals to the privates. They systematically train for reporters' presence in a way that the reporters do not train to cover the military. That control begins nearly half a world away at the Canadian Manoeuvre Training Centre (CMTC) at Camp Wainwright, Alberta, about 208 kilometres southeast of Edmonton. Every soldier who deploys to Afghanistan trains at the high-tech CMTC first.

At the CMTC, the soldiers encounter ethnic Afghan actors hired to play the role of real Afghans in theatre, living and working in very realistic mocked up villages, mosques, and markets. Soldiers who have returned from Afghanistan help with the details, which make the training second to none. The intent is to develop soldiers' expertise in dealing with the complex Afghan culture and to working through interpreters. Beginning in April 2006, a new element was added to the training; a media cell. The cell was the idea of public affairs officer Captain Tom St. Denis, a former Royal Australian Engineer who served in Vietnam. St. Denis is a former print and magazine journalist who worked in Zimbabwe, Hong Kong, and Sri Lanka before joining the Canadian Forces in 1990.[110]

Initially, Canadian commanders wanted reservists to play the role, but St. Denis convinced them that civilian journalists think differently than soldiers. His arguments won the day and the Forces hired eight journalism students for each training serial to play the role of journalists the soldiers could encounter in Afghanistan. Essentially, the media cell is a closed-circuit television facility. The students are broken into four teams of two. Two operate the facility called the Canadian News Centre, where the students' work is shaped into daily newscasts by someone like Brian Kosul, a former Manitoba newspaper editor and CBC television and radio journalist who joined the Canadian Forces in 1978 as a public affairs officer until retirement in 1993. Two students play the role of journalists with the International News Network (INN) – the mock equivalent of CNN who are unembedded. Two others play the role of local Afghan journalists with the Local Television Network (LTN), while the remaining two play the role of embedded Canadians.

During a typical exercise, the commander knows what scenario he wants his soldiers to train to, such as the reconnaissance of a market. Unknown to the soldiers, they are being set up to encounter an improvised explosive device (IED), which is detonated. The soldiers must deal, not only with the dead and wounded, but also with news reporters who show up unannounced. Such unscripted scenarios teach the soldiers how to deal with journalists seeking explanations for events they have witnessed independently and, in the case of the INN and LTN journalists, who may not be sympathetic to the

Canadians at all. Koshul explained how the training works at the tactical level.

> If the (Canadian) army says it was a successful operation, the Afghan looks around; his mother has been shot and his house burned down, from his perspective, it's not successful at all. The Canadians (embedded journalists) give the opportunity to state their (Canadian) case more than that the International News Network. The whole purpose is to train the Canadian troops. They have to be careful with the fact there is media and you do not speak above your pay grade. If they (the media) ask how an operation was planned, Joe soldier doesn't know. He (the journalist) has to go see the major. If the media ask a policy question, they say: 'Talk to the politicians.'[111]

Meanwhile Captain St. Denis explained how the media cell training works at the higher strategic level:

> The first lesson is to not let the local media seize the entire news agenda. 'If this is the coverage we're getting, we should do something about it. We can't let the bad guys get all the air time.' We can ramp up full-blown news conferences. We can exercise commanders in news conferences, for example, in handing detainees over to local authorities. We manipulate it (the news conference) to give them (commanders) experience at doing it. We tape it and we provide feedback. Here's your mannerisms; you ramble; use short sentences; do not use so much jargon.[112]

In February, 2007, the fruits of Captain (N) Chris Henderson's considerable work in the Summer 2006 *Canadian Military Journal* article on the media embedding program, and the detail which emerged in the *Toronto Star*'s Mitch Potter's reporting on the axe attack on Captain Trevor Greene, paid off. The Embedding Agreement was amended so that journalists would no longer be allowed to report the identities of soldiers who killed enemy combatants in the manner that Potter had identified Captain Schaumhn and Private McFadden, who shot Greene's assailant. Specifically, the clause reads:

> Embedded journalists will not report the identity, or specialist trades of CF personnel who kill or injure anti-coalition militants without the prior approval of the Task Force Commander....[113]

No one should doubt the efficacy of the studied and scholarly approach of the Canadian Forces toward managing the Canadian news media. There is simply no equivalent in the journalism industry.

Graham Thomson, the *Edmonton Journal*'s provincial political affairs columnist, spent six weeks embedded with the Canadian Forces in Afghanistan in the spring of 2007. Beyond the new embedding agreement (the changes to which he would have been totally unaware), he said the military's management of him during his time living and travelling with the troops was not overt; he was never once censored, but the pressure to conform to reporting acceptable to commanders and rank and file soldiers was there nonetheless. If he pushed, the military could push back with one of the hammers it held over the reporters: they could be unembedded and sent home. Thomson wrote that this was most apparent in his first news conference with the senior Canadian commander in Afghanistan, Brigadier General Tim Grant:

> In my first news conference with Brig.-Gen. Grant, he made a point of saying in front of his staff and other reporters that he had just read my last article. "And I did not like it," he said.
>
> It seems he did not appreciate how I had compared Canada's more battle-oriented mission in Afghanistan to that of the Australians' reconstruction policies. Normally, I do not mind criticism of my work and in fact have come to expect it, but these were not normal circumstances. I was a captive audience living under the thumb of the military and had just been called out by the man who had the power to have me disembedded.
>
> Nothing came of it, and a few days later Grant invited me along on a tour of the forward operating bases. But I couldn't help but feel he had just fired a warning shot across my bow.
>
> I do not think I held back as a result. When a soldier was killed in an accidental shooting, I pushed as hard as anybody to find out what happened.
>
> The military, naturally, pushed back. Embedded journalists on base thought it unfair that we weren't allowed to report on the rules governing the use of weapons at KAF. For reasons of operational security, the military did not want the enemy to know that even though all soldiers carried weapons at all times on base, the weapons aren't always loaded.
>
> Only after we complained that reporters back in Canada were freely explaining the rules in their stories did the military relent and allow embedded journalists to report that troops at KAF

did not walk around with loaded weapons all the time, information that probably eased people's minds back home when they learned KAF wasn't a ticking time bomb where weapons were ready to go off whenever somebody tripped coming out of the mess tent.[114]

Thomson wrote that a greater fear than being unembedded, however, was of writing or saying something that might get a soldier injured or killed. Journalists knew they were dependent on the rank-and-file soldiers they travelled with and whose job it was to make sure they remained alive while embedded with them. Still, as much as the journalists and soldiers learned to live together, there was friction at times. Thomson experienced that friction when Captain Kevin Megeney was accidently shot and killed on March 6, 2007. When journalists approached soldiers who knew him for details, the soldiers complained to their officers. Almost instantly, officials were at the media tent telling the reporters to leave the soldiers alone. It was implied that if they did not, they would be less welcome on future patrols outside the wire. Eventually, a compromise was reached when some soldiers agreed to talk about Corporal Megeney as long as they were not pressed for details about the accident. Thomson wrote:

> It's not the ideal situation for reporters used to much greater freedoms at home. It is not the ideal situation for the military, either, I suppose.
>
> In some ways the embedding program is a testament to the Canadian military's confidence in the professionalism of its soldiers and the value of its mission in Afghanistan. The embedding program satisfies, to a large extent, the needs of both sides. Reporters get to show Canadian's what is going on in Canada's first war since Korea. The military hopes the soldiers' stories will help win public support back home even when soldiers die in the line of duty.[115]

Thomson can be forgiven for not knowing about the Kosovo Air War in 1999 because, thanks to Canada's military commanders, no one knows much about Canada's role in that war. Still, Thomson is certain about one thing: it is only a matter of time before an embedded journalist is killed in Afghanistan. He says that not out of bravado but as a matter of fact. "Afghanistan is a dangerous place and every Canadian there, soldier or civilian, is playing Russian roulette – and pulling the trigger whenever they climb on board a convoy to head outside the wire."[116]

In June 2007, the Canadian Defence & Foreign Affairs Institute published a lengthy paper by Sharon Hobson, the Canadian correspondent for *Jane's Defence Weekly*, which expressed her opinion that the Canadian Forces and the news media rely too heavily on the embedding program as a means to tell Canadians about the mission in Afghanistan. For example, quoting un-identified journalists she had interviewed, Hobson says the Canadian Forces plays favourites among journalists who accompany them on their missions. It was not only a question of personality, but whether the military liked their previous work, or not. She wrote:

> Reporters who did go out with the troops were gambling that there would be an interesting story to tell during the course of the mission. But whether or not a reporter would be invited to go on a particular mission depended not only on available space but also on military spin and, it was strongly suspected, on personal acceptability.
>
> The military has its own public relations agenda and attempts to steer the media to particular stories. In the fall of 2006, word came down that the government wanted more reconstruction and development stories. "We've been invited on countless village medical outreach visits, ribbon-cutting ceremonies, and similar events," said one reporter.
>
> There are also attempts to block a reporter from a particular story "in which the military will promise to push a journalist out to the front lines and instead sideline the reporter in a unit that is holding a blocking position, or running a checkpoint in a safe area, or firing artillery from a distance." While the reporter concedes that such actions could be the result of happenstance, "it happens so often that I suspect it's the result of the military bureaucracy's natural inclination to choose the safest option."
>
> Another reporter who crossed swords with the military very early on in his six-week embedding assignment by filing a story the military disputed was not given any further opportunities to accompany troops outside the wire. He had not breached the ground rules, so he could not be thrown off the base, but he was essentially ostracized. In this instance, the military held all the cards, and there was no avenue of appeal.[117]

The other problem that she identified was that the journalists' editors and news directors were increasingly reluctant to commit them to missions "outside the wire," accompanying troops on operations that took them away from Kandahar Air Field for long periods of time. The reason for that attitude was that if a soldier was killed elsewhere, the journalist would not be able to cover the ramp ceremony. The airfield is the central hub through which all information flows and public affairs officers soon realized that the reporters' reluctance to go outside the wire was not their fault, but rather that of the editors and news directors back in Canada, the real gatekeepers of what Canadians could or could not know. As CBC reporter Chris Brown told her, he did not accompany the troops on operations:

> ... in part, because the places they were going to (forward operating bases mostly), simply had a lot of routine stuff going on that my desk wasn't that interested in. It is still very dangerous to go out with the military, and my feeling is that unless the desk wants a story, I'm not going to put myself and my cameraman at risk for a story they may or may not run. It has to be worthwhile.[118]

One critical issue that Hobson also touched upon in an interview with the *National Post*'s Chris Wattie, although they do not quite put it this way, is that there is an enduring belief among journalists that virtually any good reporter can cover any story. The thinking is that reporters do not have to have cancer to write a story about cancer. They do not have to be lawyers to cover courts. They do not have to be political scientists to cover politics. In fact, many journalists are rotated out of a beat after several years over for concerns that they may become too familiar with the subject material, too close to the people involved, and may lose their objectivity. The same thinking applies to journalists covering the Canadian Forces. Of the thousands employed across Canada, there are perhaps a dozen, at most, who specialize in covering the Canadian Forces. Still, more than three hundred Canadian journalists have been rotated through the embedding program for four or five weeks each since its inception. The problems they face are predictable. Most reporters show up in theatre having to learn about the complexities of the Canadian Forces, let alone Afghanistan, from scratch. The learning curve is steep. Wattie, who has been to Afghanistan several times, observed:

> "generally, news outlets are not sending their most experienced military reporters to cover this because it's an on-going, long,

drawn-out [war], and they're rotating people in and out" – often young, inexperienced people who do not recognize the import- ance of getting out into the field and gaining the trust of the troops.[119]

A number of other issues arise with that practice. While the journalists re- turn to Canada much wiser for their experience, in many cases, there is no follow-on work covering the military. The journalists go back to covering the courts and politics and, hence, any opportunity to build up a solid body of knowledge about the Canadian Forces and Afghanistan is lost. There is no collective memory. Most journalists who rotate through Afghanistan are like cats. When one leaves, the next one shows up no wiser at all for the first one being there. For a knowledge-based industry, that development is prob- lematic. Most Canadian journalists who embed with the Canadian Forces in Afghanistan are simply no match for the highly trained and experienced military public affairs officers assigned to manage them and who have seen dozens upon dozens of reporters, dozens upon dozens just like them, the soldiers on the ground who have been trained how to deal with them, or their commanders, who have also been highly coached in dealing with the news media. Add to that dynamic the imperatives of "operational security" within the embedding agreements and many journalists feel completely hamstrung. In lucid moments, they know there is nothing they can do about it. Richard Latendress experienced that himself and wrote about it in the *Calgary Sun* in September, 2007:

> Almost daily a new batch of young reporters shows up, bright eyed and bushy tailed, looking for the scoops.
>
> They find out soon enough that it is definitely a dangerous assignment, but it is one that is heavily supervised. Being embed- ded with the Canadian army gives a reporter a front-row seat on the action, and daily contact with the soldiers themselves.
>
> But, a reporter signs away part of his journalistic soul when he signs his military papers. The list of rules, restrictions and other obstacles is as long as the mission itself.
>
> We're not allowed to say exactly where we are, how many people we're with, or what equipment we have with us. Do not even think about taking pictures inside of a combat vehicle. Do not describe how a weapon works. Do not show an antenna on a hilltop where Canadian soldiers are stationed.

Although 200 Afghans go by a given command post every day here on the ground, we can't show that command post in Canada – it might be helpful to the enemy.

Do not divulge where soldiers keep their water bottles or the food rations back at the base. Bite your lip if you want to describe what the Canadians know about the enemy and its military capacity. The list goes on.

The main goal in stifling journalists is to protect our troops; do not compromise a current or future mission.

The military thinks we do. The Taliban and their henchmen are everywhere, all over the world, the Canadian military tells us repeatedly. They're watching our reports, they're reading out articles, and they're passing our word on to the big cheese, the head of the Taliban, Mullah Omar.

If the pitfalls of being embedded are annoying, the alternative is even deadlier.

You'd need a lot more than guts to drive along the roads here in your own vehicle, looking for a news story – you'd have to be rash and foolhardy. After all, the dangers threatening our soldiers threaten every outsider.

A heap of scrap metal paints a clear picture. It was an Afghan military vehicle before it met up with an improvised explosive device. I feel a lot closer travelling in a Canadian tank, thanks.

It's just a regular work day here. No one escapes the relentless sound of machine guns, rocket fire and grenade launchers.

Nor do they escape the risk of kidnapping, the latest tactic in the arsenal of the Taliban and other extremists.

With these working conditions, my choice as a reporter is clear. Despite its drawbacks, there is no wise alternative to being embedded with our soldiers.[120]

The threat to life and limb faced by the journalists, predicted by the *Edmonton Journal*'s Graham Thompson, was evidenced with the August 22, 2007, explosion of a roadside bomb that killed two Valcartier-based soldiers, Master Corporal Christian Duchesne and Master Warrant Officer Mario Mercier, who had been with Royal 22nd Regiment since July 15. Quite predictably, French Canadian journalists flocked to Afghanistan to embed with the soldiers from their home province when they deployed. Among them were Radio-Canada cameraman Charles Dubois and Patrice Roy, a Radio-Canada reporter. They were in the same armoured personnel carrier as Duchesne and Mercier when the bomb blast tore the vehicle apart. Dubois lost a leg below the knee while Roy suffered severe nervous shock. It was the first time a journalist embedded with the Forces in Afghanistan had been seriously injured. Incredibly, Roy later said that he did not understand the risks of going to Afghanistan.

> "If we'd known the operation was going to be so dangerous, we wouldn't have gone," Roy, the network's Ottawa bureau chief, said after the attack, which seriously injured his cameraman, Charles Dubois, whose leg was later amputated below the knee.
>
> "What I've been asking myself is, are the reports we want to make to explain the war worth the risks that we take and that we make our cameramen take? And I do not have an answer," Roy said in a televised interview.[121]

From a strategic perspective, the high-profile Roy's opinions were all bad news in terms of public opinion in Quebec, not only in terms of support for the war, but from a societal perspective. A CROP poll of 601 Quebecers taken before the Duschene and Mercier casualties indicated that more than two-thirds – some 68 per cent – were opposed to sending Quebec troops to Afghanistan. That was up from an earlier 57 per cent.[122] After Dubois's leg amputation, Info 690, one of Montreal's most popular AM radio stations, asked its audience in an obviously unscientific poll: "Should we continue to send journalists to Afghanistan?" At the end of the day, 60 per cent said no.[123]

That raises the troubling question that, if the war against terrorism were going well in Afghanistan, how would Quebecers know? How would they know if it was not going well in Afghanistan? Should they rely on military or government estimates of the war's progress? It is cynical to say, but Roy's opinions about journalists' roles are more reminiscent of the First World War's Max Aitken, than that of the Second World War's Ross Munro – as imperfect as his reports were – or of the Korean War's Bill Boss. The CBC's Roy did not understand the threats faced by journalists the way the *Edmonton Journal*'s Thompson did. Regardless, the Canadian Forces acted swiftly, not only in its interests, but in the embeds' interests, as well. Just five days later, journalists embedded with the Canadian Forces in Afghanistan were required to wear identity dog tags just like the soldiers. It was explained:

The Canadian military says the name tags will help make identification easier if there are any fatalities among journalists while
they are out with soldiers.

The tags "make it possible to put a name on a warm or cold
body without having to check the wallet," said Capt. Sylvain
Chalifour, a Canadian Forces spokesman.

Also, if journalists want to travel with the troops in the war-
torn country, they will have to take a first-aid course and attend
information sessions to make sure they understand the risks of
what they are doing.[124]

Clearly, after taking those steps, journalists, after August 2007, could be left
with little doubt about the risks they were taking. But, the Canadian Forces
were also being proactive in other ways. One of the most critical was by re-
defining and honing its definition of "operational security" when fighting
against insurgents. This change would have profound effects not only on
the military's role in a democracy but also on the role of the news media in a
democracy. It is imperative that the evolving nature of "operational security"
as envisioned in Defence and Administrative Orders 2008 (DAOD 2008) and
the understanding of operational security in February 14, 2008, be explained.

DAOD 2008 is the Canadian Forces' public affairs guidelines for operations effective January 30, 1998, which required the Forces to integrate public
affairs policy and direction into "all aspects of military doctrine, as appropriate, to ensure that PA is fully integrated into CF military planning, decision
making, standard operating procedures, and operations."[125] Included in
DAOD 2008, were guidelines in the event of escalating military tension or
war that required the deputy chief of defence staff to fully integrate public
affairs into military doctrine and the director general of public affairs to draft
and implement a national public affairs plan.[126]

The guidelines recognized that the key priority of any Forces operation
is to achieve its mission, but, at the same time, it accepted there would be
heightened media and public interest. The challenge for the Forces was to
inform Canadians of the national and operation dimensions "in a manner
that is accurate, complete, timely and respectful of the principles of openness, transparency and operational security."[127]

It is also clear, however, that the requirements for openness and transparency and operational security could conflict. By "operational security,"
DAOD 2008 meant "the principle of safeguarding the integrity of a military
operation or activity, and/or the safety of the CF members and other personnel involved in the military operation or activity."[128]

On February 18, 2008, at a technical briefing at National Defence Headquarters, Brigadier General Peter Atkinson, Director General Operations, Strategic Joint Staff, updated participants on Canada's activities in Afghanistan. He elaborated on the new concept of "operational security" or "opsec" in military jargon. It is imperative to examine Atkinson's interpretation because he puts it in journalistic terms, as well as the Internet, with profound consequences not only for journalists, but for Canadians whom they inform.

> Simply put, opsec is keeping the good guys' secrets from the bad guys. We firmly believe that Canadians have the right to know about our operations in Afghanistan. We also understand the importance of independent reporting and analysis of the government of Canada in this complex environment. Your appetite for information serves positive and lawful objectives of our Canadian democracy. Opsec allows the safeguarding of some information that has an operational impact on our mission while permitting Canadians to know as much as possible about their soldiers and members of the whole government team.
>
> I described recently, at the Standing Committee on National Defence, the mosaic effect as it relates to operational security. This can be portrayed in terms of journalism. A news story is not complete until all facets of it are discovered and reported. It leads off with a tip to a potential story. The journalist then pursues a lead to put a comprehensive story together that portrays the result of all their sources.
>
> In essence, the mosaic effect is just that. Simply, the smallest piece of information may be invaluable in the hands of personnel employed in the counter intelligence world, given the fact that they have access to a much broader spectrum of information. In the hands of a journalist, unrelated pieces of information can be turned into an excellent story.
>
> The same is true for sensitive information, which may not in and of themselves be sensitive but formed together they create a comprehensive picture of significant use to our adversaries. To provide some context, a current example from our ongoing mission in Afghanistan may help.
>
> The CDS described this about a week ago, when he was in front of the media. The Taliban put a huge amount of effort to find out where their people have gone when they disappear.

They do not know whether they've been killed, they do not know whether they've been detained. They do not know when they show back up whether they've simply been released because of a lack of evidence or if they show back up it's because they've turned and are reporting to us.

They do not know whether they're giving us information when they've been detained and they put a huge effort into finding this out, to try and determine those things. At the same time, they find it very difficult to peel back what happened and look at our tactics and, therefore, make us more predictable to them, and therefore increase the risk to our soldiers on the ground. This is the operational security aspect of it. It causes the Taliban great difficulty. And we're comfortable with that because we've got a responsibility to our soldiers and to their families.

So, from a whole of government perspective, the overarching opsec principle is a collective responsibility for all of us both military, civilian, our families and I would say even the media. In a recent case, a media outlet understood opsec and made the right choice. The outlet asked for specific details on a mission's rules of engagement and about our contingency plan.

The Canadian Forces discussed the request with the specific media outlet, explaining that providing the information to that level of detail would have placed our troops at risk. The outlet agreed and they did not pursue the request and that mission went off without a hitch.

Now, the internet specifically. Social networking sites like Facebook. It's an invaluable tool for our soldiers to stay in contact with their families and friends. To the same degree, the internet is a fertile environment for exploitation. Sharing sites like YouTube and the collaborative Wiki type sites make exploitation very easy. A practical example from the internet is a useful demonstration of what I'm talking about.

A search of the text "Canadian deaths in Afghanistan" resulted in approximately 200,000 hits. They range from accredited media agencies to Wikipedia to personal blogs. The mosaic effect is perfectly illustrated by the Wikipedia site. Due to its collaborative content contribution anybody can add to the content, providing a compilation of details on a specific instance. For example, like the description of a casualty with photos, locations and news articles contributed by several sources.

The insurgents could use this information to determine their success or their lack of it, of their actions, and determine better ways for them to attack us. Because of the speed and capacity of today's technology, we are virtually providing the enemy with his battle damage assessment instantly.

To close, here is an excerpt from an Al-Qaeda training manual with respect to their use of information sources. They identify that an organization must gather as much information as possible about the enemy, in other words about us. Information in their words has two sources. Public sources. Using this public source openly and without reporting to illegal means it is possible to gather at least 80% of the information about the enemy.

Now secret sources. It is possible through these secret and dangerous methods to obtain 20% of the information that is considered secret. So we need to make their collection efforts as difficult as possible, by denying them 80% of the solution. This will make it difficult for groups like Al-Qaeda to plan their operations.[129]

Brigadier General Atkinson clearly believes with almost messianic zeal in the imperatives of operational security and his thoughts would be acceptable if he lived in a totalitarian state. Canada is a democracy. It is not the place of a Canadian military man, regardless of his sincerity, to suggest that the publicly available information about Canada's prosecution of the war against terrorism in Afghanistan should be denied to Canadians in the news and to Al-Qaeda as a by-product. The public's right to know is not worth the life of even one Canadian soldier, but at the same time, one of the values that a military man living in a democracy ought to defend – not obliterate in the name of operational security – is the democratic role of the news media, even when it comes to Afghanistan. Yet, there are many within the Canadian Forces who see the news media as enemy, as it will be seen presently.

Public Affairs Officers

Whether stationed at home or abroad, military public affairs officers play a contested role in facilitating, managing, shaping, or censoring the news and the journalists who produce it, depending on the perspective. Major Jay Janzen, who wrote the *Canadian Army Journal* on the initial success of the embedding program after his experience in Afghanistan, is among them. That article, he explained, was written for mid-level commanders to demonstrate that the news media can be managed well and relations between the military and the media can go easier if it is done right. Janzen was assigned the public affairs officer in Kabul during the first major rotation of Canadian battle group from August 2003, to February 2004. When he first arrived in Afghanistan, there were no embedded ground rules in place because they had not yet been approved in Ottawa. That immediately placed him in conflict with Canadian journalists at the gates of Camp Julien, the Canadian compound. Among them was the *National Post*'s Chris Wattie, who lodged a formal complaint. For about a week to ten days, Janzen said there was nothing he could do to accommodate them. Finally, the journalists were allowed in and the deputy commander of the International Security Assistance Force (ISAF) took a personal interest in accommodating them as much as he could, Janzen said.

> At that time, we were still a post-Somalia culture and there were folks in the senior NCO corps who would consider the media almost to be enemy i.e. the sergeants and the warrant officers. When the senior warrant officers aren't media friendly, it can make an impact on the young guys. For the media to come in and live with us was tough post-Somalia. But, General Leslie realized we weren't going to succeed in the mission and with the Canadian public without the media. The media was to be welcomed and not excluded, but included. That was a shift in the way of thinking for some people. So, when the troops come into the mess hall and see the commanding officer sitting with two or three journalists and having a conversation, that says something to the troops.[130]

Clearly, Brigadier General Atkinson is in the camp that views the news media as enemy. Major Janzen, meanwhile, explained that perhaps a dozen Canadian journalists, at most, specialize in covering the Canadian Forces. It is possible, he said, to count the number of journalists who have covered the Canadian Forces for twenty years or more on one hand. Janzen said it was the more experienced journalists who tended to be the first to arrive in Afghanistan. Among them were the Canadian Press's Steven Thorne and Les Perreaux, the *National Post*'s Matthew Fisher, and CBC television reporters Steve Chow and Rob Gordon. Janzen said he saw Thorne take a number of young journalists from the *Sun* newspaper chain under his wing and show them the ropes.

> But, when the vets rotated out, we had people there who did not know the rank structure, who did not know the difference between a colonel and a corporal. We had people with no money looking for an ATM machine. A lot did not show up with Flak jackets and helmets. When we had several inches of snow in December and temperatures below zero, we had people show up with no sleeping bags. We had freelancers show up from small community newspapers, who in some cases did not have proper clearance from Ottawa. They just showed up. Of course we took them in, but now we're more strict [*sic*]. They have to get the proper clearance before they get on the plane.[131]

One Canadian Forces public affairs officer admitted to this author off the record that it was preferred that the media embed with the Forces in Afghanistan for six weeks for a very specific reason. Most show up not knowing a lot about either the military or Afghanistan and it takes them about six weeks to get up to speed. During that time, they take direction from public affairs officers readily, but after six weeks, they develop their own ideas about what they want to cover, which is not always in the Forces' best interest.[132] Janzen, however, disagreed. He explained that, over time, the military saw that over the course of non-stop work in Afghanistan, seven days a week, many journalists become tired and burn out.

> It's for a good reason we do the six weeks. There is a lot of stress and they do not necessarily have the training and unit support of the Forces. Six weeks with us is an intense indoctrination. They're eating with us; living with us; getting shot at. It's like being immersed in a new culture. In many cases, they're a lone wolf out there. Their families do not have military family resource centres backing them up. I know people from small papers who went there who would never come back and would never cover defence again. And the news media is changing, going to smaller staffs and downsizing. The media guys who have been there before, they're confident and they'll tell you what they want and you take them and put them in with units. But when you get someone who is green and from the smaller papers, quite often

they're overwhelmed. You've got to hold their hand. They get lost
in camp; they can't find the showers and the mess hall. They're
overwhelmed by the danger and the thousands of troops. They're
just overwhelmed.[133]

Time and again, Janzen said, the public affairs officers saw new inexperienced journalists repeat the same pattern. Many would be reluctant to go on
patrols in the dangerous hinterlands outside the main camp.

After a few days, they think they can't trust the public affairs officers. They wouldn't go on patrol, but at the same time they had
something to prove. There are rules about soldiers not fraterniz-
ing in theatre, even husbands and wives. But there was specula-
tion about who might be, so they would write these trivial stories
about sex in the camp. It seemed like once they got that out of
their system they would relax and they would say (to the public
affairs officers): 'What would you like to do now?' I always get the
sense that some journalists are always looking for the big scoop.
When I say that: the next Somalia scandal. It wasn't what we were
doing on the ground; it was what we were doing wrong. Look at
the detainee file. On that whole file there's many people working
to try to find some wrong doing. We saw the British soldiers beat-
ing children in Iraq in 2005 and the Americans in Abu Ghraib
(prison). The damage that causes is almost irreparable. But one
of the reasons we've got the support of the Canadian people,
whether it's support for the mission or the troops, one of the big
reasons the Canadian Forces enjoy the public support is because
the troops on the ground are conducting themselves in an exem-
plary manner.[134]

Major Janzen acknowledges in the *Canadian Army Journal* article that the
embedding program enables the military to influence news media coverage,
but he says there is a big difference between influencing the news media
coverage and "spinning" the journalists and their news so that the Canadian
Forces are depicted in an positive light.

It's a question of, we have the information, you decide what to
do with it. We do not make a concerted effort to distort or shape
or influence public opinion. It's not cloak and dagger stuff. We're

trained to set the conditions for humanitarian aid and the rule of law [in Afghanistan] so little girls go to school. The bottom line is we do good work.[135]

This was precisely the point that a *Globe and Mail* article made on June 4, 2008, that that direction had been given and military public affairs officers promoted stories about the Forces enabling development work. Regardless, Janzen also addressed the issue of operational security and his approach to it. He acknowledged that the Forces do withhold information but he said 95 per cent of the time it is for reasons of operational security and that, if it were released, someone could get killed. The information could also be classified. But, on the other hand, he said, there was a strong contingent of soldiers in Afghanistan who did not want to be identified in news reports, fearing their families might be targeted in Canada. (This was precisely the erroneous reasons airmen were not identified during the 1999 Kosovo Air War.) Janzen said:

> They wanted to use nicknames and pseudonyms. The first question I raised was: is this a credible threat? I went to the CF intelligence branch to up the chain of command at NDHQ. That was July 2003. The answer was: No. There is no credible threat. There were occupations like snipers we had classified, but soldiers are encouraged to use their full names. It lends credibility to the mission, but we do not force any soldier to give his name or do interviews with the media, just do not say you're not allowed to. If they are asked how many insurgents you have killed, the answer is taking lives is an unfortunate part of what we do, but we do not want to set people up for retribution.[136]

At Camp Nathan Smith in Kandahar, Afghanistan, Captain Joanne Blais was the public affairs officer for the Kandahar Provincial Reconstruction Team in December 2007. She had worked in public affairs at both Kandahar Air Field from October to November 2006 and at the KRP in December 2006 and then returned to KAF and worked with the battle group, replacing its public affairs officer. She says she sees many similar behaviours in journalists who arrive in Afghanistan for the first time.

> I find that when you have a reporter in a harsh environment, he wants to go back and say he covered a war. They're war

correspondents in their minds; the faster they get outside Kandahar Air Field, the better feel they have for how it works. They have to be out there and sleep with the soldiers and then they know what they want. They're all hyperactive and they're afraid they will not deliver. Then, they're a lot more relaxed and know what they're looking for. They can tell the people at home they were out there with the soldiers.[137]

She said that, on many occasions, journalists want stories on non-combat reconstruction aspects of the provincial development team, but they have no idea what stories are out there, who to talk to, or even where to start. As a result, Blais directs them to the Women's Literary Program, a Civil Military Co-operation (CIMIC) team or the World Food Program.

With the literary program, they have to go with a fixer. So I try to find them an opportunity and we call the Canadian embedded journalist. We have an activity for you Friday at 9 a.m. Some reporters will not go with a fixer. They're afraid of kidnapping. The other one I work with is the CIMIC team. I would offer a reporter the chance to spend a week with the military in a *shura* [a meeting with village elders]. It's not perfect. I still send them outside the wire for a week, but when they come back I know what types of projects they are interested in covering. They also do not have the contacts here in the city with the World Food Program. So they come to us and say these are the things I am interested in, can you help me out?[138]

Blais acknowledges that there can be both upsides and downsides to offering journalists opportunities to go outside the wire, because, if they do, their editors will be furious if a soldier dies and they are not there to cover the ramp ceremonies. On the one hand, if they go outside the wire, they will be in the middle of the action. On the other, in the event of fatalities, she tries to assure them they can be returned in time for the ramp ceremony. Having said that, there are technical problems why some journalists cannot remain at the provincial reconstruction team for long. There are no television facilities at the PRT location on the north side of Kandahar City. Television reporters must return to the airfield to file their stories while print reporters can file from almost anywhere by internet or satellite telephone. But, Blais also notes a host of other issues that she has observed either when journalists first arrive or they are about to leave:

> I find they're not physically prepared for the challenge. We ask: "Could they walk three kilometres with a sleeping bag on their back?" One guy was overweight and he couldn't fit in the back of a LAV (Light Armoured Vehicle). It's hard to find somebody physically fit for the challenge. I also do not like to have them at the end of the six weeks. They're tired and they do not care anymore. What are we going to do, kick them out? That's when they get opsec information out. But the same thing happens with the military. After five and a half months, a lot of accidents happen. You're tired.[139]

The other problem that she discovered accommodating some journalists' request about aid stories is that it could take four days to get permission from a Canadian International Development Agency director in Ottawa to write about a story. For example, it was essential to send Timothea Gibb to work with her at Camp Nathan Smith because the embedded journalists prefer to interview people in person.

Gibb is a public diplomacy officer who handles the media relations and requests relating to CIDA and Department of Foreign Affairs and International Trade programs. Of the 250 Canadian journalists who have been embedded in Afghanistan, she has observed, it is always the same ones who return more than once: CTV's Steve Chow, Murray Oliver, and Paul Workman; the *Globe and Mail*'s Graeme Smith and Christie Blatchford, and Canadian Press's Bill Graveland. Graveland, in particular, likes to be where the action is, she said:

> Like one time I sent him out with the OMLET [Operational Mentor Liaison Team]. They were shot at. He said it was great; we got a lot of action. And others will come back and say, if I knew it was going to be that dangerous, I wouldn't go. My task is to get the development and reconstruction story out. What I learned with many of our development programs do not want a military convoy to come out here. The trick was to send media with fixers like staff. I look to see who is willing to entertain reporters and then they come back to get Canadian content. It's tough. A lot of them work until 2 or 3 a.m. in the morning so they can file their stories on time with the 9 ½ hours' time difference. You have to

manage their stress, as well. It isn't easy. I completely understand. Our schedule doesn't give them much time to sleep.[140]

Journalists

At the time of writing, the Canadian Press's Bill Graveland had been to Afghanistan twice. The first time was from November, 2006, to January 15, 2007, and the second time from October 19 to December 5, 2007. He noticed striking differences between his first and second assignments. He travelled mostly with the Princess Patricia's Canadian Light Infantry and the Lord Strathcona's Horse (Royal Canadians), a tank regiment on his first assignment, but on his second assignment, the French Canadian Royal 22nd Regiment was in theatre.

> The first time there was a lot of media. There was twelve to four-teen, so there was a lot of competition. The PAFFOs would come with an opportunity. They would say how would you like to go with PsyOps (psychological operations) foot patrolling? They'd be looking for a story on PsyOps and they would generally disguise it with something classified. For example, when I went with the Psyops guys, it was their first time deploying tanks at Masum Ghar, near Panjwaii, but they knew they were coming over so they got me and CTV to cover the story at the same time. It was a publicity bonus for them and a nice story for us.
>
> They always come to us with something in mind, so you would get that story to pick up as well as a dozen others just being there. Back then, there was no restrictions, you could name the forward operating bases, Masum Ghar, Sperwan Ghar. It was a lot more relaxed. They might come by to tell you this is a little wrong or the name of the regiment is wrong. They read everything. I must have interviewed General (Tim) Grant a half a dozen times at least and Col. Omar Lavoie. They were accessible all the time, constantly. Generally, if you want to go out constantly, they treat it differently. I went out 10 or 12 times so generally, if you want things, they would make it happen.
>
> The second time, in August, there would have been sixteen or eighteen there. It was packed. They had an extra media tent to sleep in. At the time, the PAFFO made it clear to me that the English media were second fiddle to the French media. But there

ended up being remarkably less media. Perhaps half a dozen and there were a lot more restrictions. After the Radio Canadian cameraman lost his leg, most of the Francophone media left after the first three or four weeks. After that, there were six of us, *The Globe and Mail* and the TV pool. November 6 they started doing the television pool: CTV, CBC and Global. They decided to go to the pool system because of costs.[141]

Graveland was at Forward Operating Base (FOB) Wilson on November 17, 2007, when National Defence Minister Peter MacKay arrived and rockets were fired at the base. He said the media were kept at a different part of the base when the rocket attack happened. After the rocket attack, the media were censured, for operational security reasons, for identifying FOB Wilson. Suddenly, he said, it was difficult for any of them to make trips outside the wire.

Then they started clamping down. In the Arghandab region, the Taliban tried to take care of a leadership vacuum. The mullah died of a heart attack. Previously, they would let us go forward. They had briefings at the base, but they wouldn't let us go forward. I did a story on unmanned aerial vehicles and talked to the soldiers inside the mission, the captain and the major who gave us information. They could see the Taliban guys, but they couldn't get air support in quickly enough. You could see the Taliban and the RPGs. It looked like they were ten feet away. They called in air support to blow the shit out of them, but it did not show up. The soldiers were expressing concern that if we had a Predator, they'd be dead by now. I purposely didn't name the soldiers because I thought there might be repercussions. The next day, I'm called into the head public affairs officer who was not pleased with the story. They tried to say it was operational security, but it wasn't. The soldiers thanked me for it saying it was right on, but I got dressed down for it. I said, they did you a favour, this machine is a piece of shit. The next time I did a story, there was a public affairs officer sitting in. I said: "This is new," and he said: "No, we always do this." It's incredible the extent of the restrictions.[142]

Without a doubt, the most prominent Canadian journalist in Afghanistan was the *Globe and Mail*'s Graeme Smith, who first began travelling there from Russia in 2005 when he was assigned to the *Globe*'s Moscow bureau, ostensibly from 2005 to 2007. At the time, he was told Afghanistan would be 20 per cent of his job. He wrote a proposal arguing it should be 100 per cent of his job. As a result, Smith was assigned permanently to Afghanistan in the summer of 2006 until spring 2009. With nineteen weeks a year off by agreement, he did not get paid any extra for one of the most dangerous assignments on earth. For example, in November 2006, he tried an experiment to report on Afghanistan independently from the Canadian Forces.

> I rented an office compound on the south side of Kandahar. Then in February 2007, three gun men raided the place. Two had AK-47s and one had a pistol. No one was there but my cook who got beat up. There was a lap top computer and a couple of disks. They searched the place pretty thoroughly from top to bottom. Military intelligence told me it was directed at me; it was the fact they didn't steal the computer. It could have been two things, intimidation and kidnapping. We talked to the Taliban later and they said it wasn't them. It was a short-lived experiment. It was lovely to have a meeting place to invite people for tea. We did a story on the economy and unemployment. There was a street where guys were hanging out looking for jobs. Instead of hanging out on the street, we invited them in for tea. You don't just walk up to somebody on the street in Kandahar.[143]

Smith says he has seen dramatic changes in the way the military treats and manages the news media over the years as a result of political direction from Ottawa.

> There has been a massive shift in military PR strategy. In 2005, it was all access; all you can eat. When I first arrived in Kandahar, they gave me an intelligence briefing on what was going on. In 2006, the media arrived en masse and the media were clawing each other's eyes out to go on a convoy. There was a lot of mistrust. We weren't sure how the game was being played. The military learned in 2006 that if they gave us lots and lots of access, we would tell their story, rather than someone else's. Before Operation Medusa, the Royal Canadian Regiment got it. They

pushed us over to the front all the time, which was a double edged sword. We glossed over civilian casualties. We didn't really cover that because we were out with the troops. That was a PR coup for the military. Canadians knew what was going on. They saw the operations. Then the news cycle cooled down in 2007. It was still all access, you could go on as many patrols as you wanted, but they started to become concerned about spin. A public affairs captain started coming out to the field, supervising you.

There was a message from up high that we were getting sloppy on opsec, using names we used for roads; these bizarre situations. A top general would describe opening Route Fosters, it runs parallel to the Arghandab River and Panjwaii. They thought route was another name for a road, so we had to redo the clip saying The Road. It's not security, just a restriction of information. If they could keep us worried about roads and things then presumably they could keep us worrying about other things. They told me it came from Ottawa, the Centre; the Privy Council Office.[144]

Working in Kandahar, Smith was basically confined to KAF at night. No one has an independent base outside the wire. He employed two full-time fixers. One handled the government contacts and the other, who had relatives in the Taliban, handled tribal and Taliban contacts. As part of Smith's daily routine, he woke up in an eight-man tent at the Kandahar Air Field. If he wanted to unembed, he dressed in local Afghan clothes and walked across the stones that lead to the airfield base's entrance. In 2007, he says, it was safe enough to walk the local streets at night. He also drove a beat-up Toyota Corolla.

Last winter I was driving 40 kilometres outside of the city. In the spring, I wouldn't leave the central part of the city. There is a journalistic credo; do not get killed for colour. If you do cover some UN agencies, the risk is getting targeted. You have to ask if it's worthwhile. I'm not concerned about getting blown up; I worried about kidnapping. I try to be back by dusk because it's getting dangerous out there.

I can go downtown on any given day. I can unembed and get a taxi. But there is a rule: you have to spend the majority of your time covering the Canadian military. On more than one occasion, I've been told they can kick me out because I spend a lot of time downtown. I said: "A) let me know when I write a story that doesn't have to do with Canadians or B) kick me out and let's see what happens."[145]

In that regard, Smith says he was under pressure – and often threat – from both the Afghan government and the Canadian Forces.

> If I write a story about the environment minister that he doesn't like, he might not talk to me again. If we write a story about a governor that he doesn't like, the Canadian Forces tell us we're threatened with violence. You have to do a risk assessment for everything you do. I've been told there are stories I shouldn't write until I'm permanently ready to leave. I think what we're doing in Afghanistan is flawed but, if we leave, things will be worse. My basic thinking is the West has come to Afghanistan and tried to do too much with too little. All of this is with the caveat that I'm a reporter and I have to keep an open mind.[146]

There are two last points that, as a journalist, Smith says he was certain about. The first point is that he made a wise decision to stop taking lessons in Pashto, the Iranian language spoken mostly in Afghanistan. He explained:

> I was learning it, but I made a conscious decision to stop learning. I don't want Afghanistan to become my life. It's a tough, tough place. I know journalists who have made it their life and I think they're fucking insane. You have to push yourself. I'm going to be doing this for the next 18 months or two years. Foreigners, in general, don't understand how dangerous Afghanistan is. Things have gotten worse but that doesn't mean it's hopeless. People confuse things that are drastically worse and completely hopeless.[147]

The second thing about which he was absolutely certain is that the war is Canada's single most important foreign policy issue. In that regard, he says:

> It's a failing of the Canadian media that I'm the only guy permanently assigned there. There should be an army of us over there.[148]

If the Canadian Press's Graveland[149] and the *Globe and Mail*'s Smith are anomalies in Canadian journalism for their ongoing commitment to covering Afghanistan, the *Calgary Herald*'s Renata D'Aliesio is far more typical of the some three hundred who have been embedded with the Canadian Forces there. D'Aliesio was the *Herald*'s environmental reporter who, years earlier, had taken a week-long course in conflict reporting offered for insurance reasons in Vancouver by CanWest, while at the *Edmonton Journal* in 2003. She recalled:

> The first three days it was gunshot wounds and we went through what you do to get a fixer and how to use a satellite phone, but it wasn't conflict training like you would get from a military or private firm. Because I had taken the training, my (*Herald*) editor asked me if I was willing to go to Afghanistan. CanWest had decided to start staffing Afghanistan on four to six week rotations. I knew when I went to Afghanistan, to tell the story properly, I had to leave the wire. I was prepared to do that.[150]

D'Aliesio arrived in Kabul, Afghanistan, on Monday September 4, 2006. By Wednesday, she had flown to Kandahar. She had time for a quick helicopter tour of the area with Canadian Brigadier General David Fraser, head of NATO's southern Afghanistan operation, and to write one story about a married couple of soldiers at Kandahar Air Field, to be published on Friday September 8. She was given notice on Thursday evening at 11 p.m. that, if she wanted to embed for Operation Medusa, she should be ready for 5 a.m. Operation Medusa was an offensive in southern Afghanistan against an estimated 3,000 to 4,000 Taliban fighters and involved some 6,000 NATO troops from five countries in addition to Afghan forces.[151] She knew that her competition, the *Globe and Mail*'s Graeme Smith and the Canadian Press's Les Perreaux were already in the field with the troops and she felt duty-bound to take whatever risks were necessary to report on the OP Medusa. She accompanied General Fraser to a Canadian staging point at Forward Operating Base Wilson and met up with Captain Ed Stewart of A company with the Princess Patricia's from Winnipeg. She was told she would be out a day or two but was out nearly ten days. She recalled:

> It was a lot of learning as I went. I'm originally from Toronto and I think I was thankful that I went camping when I moved to Alberta. The first couple of days, they were waiting to get orders to advance. That was good because I didn't understand the military structure. I got to know some of the soldiers and that I could handle the hardship, sleeping in the sand and being up that many hours. They got to know me. One thing, being a female,

you had to let go of a lot of your vanity. They wouldn't let me to go the bathroom, to the bush, alone. I had to ask for an armed escort. I had let go, but one of the concerns was here was this extra person they had to worry about. But, I found the explosions happening around you, it took a couple of days to stop jumping and sleep through that.

The first night, they wanted me to sleep in the LAV, but I wanted to sleep outside and they let me but, when it got too dangerous, they made me sleep inside. When they were advancing on foot to the village, I wanted to go, but they wouldn't let me, so there were limitations. But, as I spent time with them, as a reporter, I started realizing it was too risky. When they went into Pashmul, they wouldn't let me in until it was safe. I briefly had a sense of where I was on the map. People ask me, did I see bodies? No. I was inside the LAV when they were fighting, but you have no sense of the fighting. At that point, they had already suffered initial casualties and their tactics had changed. They decided to get more aggressive. When they got into Pashmul, they were surprised there were so few Taliban. After a couple of days, I realized I could take it. At that point, Graeme and Les decided to go back and I was the only one with A company. They switched me to a company from Petawawa that was staying outside Pashmul.[152]

Long gone are the days when Second World War correspondents like Ross Munro had to wait until he returned to London from the beaches at Dieppe to file his stories, or two days for Bill Boss's story on Kap'yong to be published. After D'Aliesio finished her research and interviews, she plugged her computer into the soldiers' Light Armoured Vehicle's electrical system. Aiming her satellite phone into position, she accessed the Internet through her laptop and filed her stories. As the soldiers watched her go about her work, they warmed up to her.

They told me it was good for morale to have me with them. They have a few women, but it's not the same. It was refreshing for the soldiers to have someone who was not military. It got them connected to the outside world. I realized how much better it was to do my job out in the field than on base where people are scared to talk to you. I know a lot of them were surprised you were willing to go through it as much as we did. It was kind of

cool. The soldiers were asking me: "Are you getting paid better to
be here?" and I said: "Nope, I'm getting the same money as writing about the environment in Calgary." That's when they think
you're crazy.[153]

D'Aliesio said breaking operational security was never an issue during
Operation Medusa because the soldiers simply would not tell her what they
were going to do next. After Medusa, she spent a week back at Kandahar Air
Field and then opted to go back into the field with a provincial reconstruction team. She stayed with them in Zhari district where, in earlier fighting,
Canadian Special Forces and the Afghan military had killed some five hundred Taliban at Sperwan Ghar, but the embedding ground rules would not
let her write about the Special Forces. When General Rick Hillier showed up
to address the troops, he did not know D'Aliesio was there and told them
about plans to strengthen the LAVs and went into the details. When he saw
D'Aliesio, he personally told her she could not report that fact for operational
security reasons. She left the details out of her story. At that point, her power
adaptor broke and she ended up dictating stories. At times, there was also
conflict with the rank and file soldiers she met at Kandahar Air Field.

> We were on base when a suicide bomber hit A company. They
> were on this foot patrol. Four of them died. We were trying to
> talk to the soldiers when they returned and we got reamed out
> for that. They said you can't talk to anyone for 24 to 48 hours.
> Then they realized it was part of our job to talk to soldiers and
> they decided they would talk to us. The military has learned to
> offer someone up to speak to issues.[154]

D'Aliesio says that it was not until she arrived in Dubai after six weeks in
Afghanistan that the enormity of what she had just done started to sink in.
And, as a result of Afghanistan, she said she learned a lot about herself. Her
reflections on that experience echo Janzen's observations that journalists
often do not have the support network that the military does and that, in
many cases, they can feel like lone wolves.

> It wasn't until I got to Dubai that I realized the stress I was under.
> I realized how little fear I had out there, which was bad because I
> started taking risks. I went to Sperwan Ghar in a G-wagon with
> Canadian soldiers, military policemen, on a dirt road that was

known to be packed with explosives. They were scared the whole time and I realized how scared they were. We made it okay, but I later realized that was a risk I probably shouldn't have taken, but soldiers were doing it every day.

You know that something could happen to you; you could get injured and you could die. I also realized that I'm tougher than I thought. But you're back in quiet Calgary, there is this feeling, I'm going to be okay doing stories here. [In Afghanistan] you were involved in the biggest story in the whole world, but you don't have anyone here who understands. All those things I was grappling with; if I could go back, I would, now knowing I would better understand.[155]

Operation Medusa

For sixteen days in September, 2006, Canadian soldiers participated in one of its largest sustained ground battles since the Second World War, Operation Medusa, against 3,000 to 4,000 Taliban fighters.[156] Precise numbers of NATO soldiers from the participating countries have not been revealed, but it was generally reported that hundreds of Canadian troops were involved. The battles took place in the Zhari, Panjwaii, and Pashmul regions that had been used as Taliban staging grounds for terror attacks and ambushes in and around Kandahar City, some thirty kilometres to the east. In the preceding four months, fighting in these regions had claimed the lives of six Canadian soldiers and left dozens more wounded. In keeping with the news media dictum "If it bleeds, it leads" news of the pitched battles was guaranteed front-page coverage when four Canadians were killed on September 3, one day after the battle started. The operation ended on Sunday, September 17. As such, Operation Medusa offers a rich case study opportunity to compare and contrast the coverage of eight select Canadian English-language newspapers from Vancouver to Halifax of the combat operation and the manifestations of the media embedding program. Each newspaper's coverage was examined in its entirety from September 2 through to September 18, the day after combat operations ceased. These newspapers represent two distributed nationally, major markets in the west and central Canada, medium markets on the prairies and a minor market newspaper on Canada's east coast. The newspapers' coverage examined below is presented in alphabetical order.

Calgary Herald

From September 3 to 18, the *Herald* ran thirty-nine news stories and three opinion pieces about Afghanistan. Of them, eighteen originated in Afghanistan and thirteen were authored by Renata D'Aliesio, the *Herald* staff writer in Afghanistan who was embedded with the troops during Operation Medusa. Her first story appeared on September 9, the result of her arrival in theatre after the operation began. Given the nature of the insurgent battle, she never had the opportunity to witness the epic confrontations between Allies and enemies that Ross Munro and Bill Boss did during the Second World War and Korea respectively. When there was combat or danger, the soldiers kept her ensconced inside their Light Armoured Vehicle. However, D'Aliesio was undoubtedly risking her life following the soldiers on patrol and taking pictures of them in one of the most heavily mined areas in the world, where most soldiers do not die in combat but as a result of improvised explosive devices. Most of her stories were about what the soldiers she was with found after the battles were over, their thoughts on the conflict, and on the firefights they had been in. The vast majority of stories in the *Herald* during that period dealt with the political fall-out from four Canadians killed by rocket propelled grenades on the first day of battle, Sunday, September 3. It was front-page news and it was followed by a steady stream of news and comment when the coffins returned to Canada and their funeral services were held. September 11th, the fifth anniversary of the 9/11 attacks on the World Trade Centre in New York, sparked most of the coverage with tributes paid to the Canadians who had lost their lives in Afghanistan in the following years. The New Democratic Party also held a convention in Quebec at about the same time, and party leader Jack Layton's call for a pull-out of Canadian troops from Afghanistan also dominated coverage. Prime Minster Stephen Harper was quoted in just one 9/11 news story in which he drew links to it and Canada's role in Afghanistan. D'Aliesio wrapped up her coverage of Operation Medusa in interviews on its success with Brigadier General David Fraser, the Canadian commander of NATO in southern Afghanistan and Kandahar's Governor Asadullah Khalid.

National Post (Toronto)

The *National Post*, owned by CanWest, is one of two Canadian daily newspapers distributed nationally. Over the course of Operation Medusa, it carried nineteen news stories related to Afghanistan. Only five articles originated in Afghanistan with the majority authored from Ottawa. Most of the stories centred on the troops who died, including a friendly-fire incident on September 4 in which two U.S. jets erroneously strafed Canadians in Operation Medusa, killing one and injuring dozens. That incident followed the deaths of four Canadians in combat, ensuring a steady stream of comment on Afghan fatalities, what could be done to prevent them, and the New Democratic Party's call for a pull-out of Canadians from Afghanistan at its party convention. Prime Minister Stephen Harper figured prominently in only one news story relating to Sept. 11 and its link to Canada's role in Afghanistan. The *Post* carried two news stories by CanWest affiliate, the *Calgary Herald*'s Renata D'Aliesio, about a school that had been reduced to rubble during Operation Medusa and a wrap-up story on Medusa's success in which she quoted Asadullah Khalid, the Governor of Kandahar province, from a news conference.

The Chronicle-Herald (Halifax)

The *Chronicle-Herald* carried twenty-three news stories and one opinion piece related to Afghanistan during Operation Medusa. Most of the ten stories originating from Afghanistan were authored by the Canadian Press's Les Perreaux and centred on the deaths of the five Canadians killed early in the operation. The balance of stories authored in Canada focused on the grieving families, NATO's call for more troops in Afghanistan, and the NDP's call for a withdrawal of Canadian troops from Afghanistan. Prime Minister Stephen Harper figured in just one 9/11 story and its links to Canada's war on terror. It also carried a Canadian Press story by Les Perreaux on September 18 about the success of Operation Medusa.

The Gazette (Montreal)

Of the thirty-five news stories and one opinion piece carried by the *Gazette* during Operation Medusa, thirteen were datelined from Afghanistan. Of them, six, or almost half, were authored by Renata D'Aliesio of its CanWest affiliate the *Calgary Herald*, who wrote about the soldiers' thoughts of taking lives, their occupation of abandoned Taliban strongholds, and farmers resuming their daily activities. The vast majority of stories dealt with soldiers' deaths, families remembering them, funerals, and, not surprisingly, the New Democratic convention held in Quebec City, which called for the pull-out of Canadian troops from Afghanistan. The fact the convention was in Quebec City made it a natural draw for a Montreal newspaper. Prominent references to Prime Minister Harper included his linkage of the 9/11 attacks and Canada's Afghan mission. There was no wrap-up story on Medusa's success. Rather, the last story written during its timeframe argued the Canadian deaths were far greater than American, quoting the left-wing Centre for Policy Alternatives.

The Globe and Mail

The Globe and Mail, also distributed nationally, carried forty-seven news stories about Afghanistan during Operation Medusa, eight opinion pieces, three editorials, and one analysis piece. Seventeen of the news stories were datelined Afghanistan. Of these, sixteen were authored by Graeme Smith. Smith was clearly in the thick of things in Medusa from the beginning. When four Canadians were killed on the first day of battle, his report was the only one that included reaction from a Taliban fighter. Smith managed to file a remarkably detailed report of Canadians advancing on insurgents under bright moonlight and later engaging four Taliban fighters, calling in helicopter support and rocket fire and, ultimately, the 25-millimetre gun on Major Geoff Abthorpe's LAV 3, "destroying" an AK-47-wielding insurgent on September 6. Otherwise, his coverage followed a pattern of reporting on the Canadians killed and others wounded by an accidental American strafing; although he did report on other combat operations, the reports of deaths were sanitized as numbers only. The balance of the Globe's coverage was largely written in Ottawa and Toronto as localized follow-ups to his reports, and news and analysis of the New Democratic Party's stand on pulling the troops out of Afghanistan. Editorially, the newspaper tore into then-Defence Minister Gordon O'Connor, who told the Reuters news service in Australia that NATO needed more troops in Afghanistan. The newspaper said that Canadians needed to be far better informed about the Afghan mission than by learning about it from O'Connor half a world away. The newspaper was also the first to correctly report on Canada sending fifteen Leopard tanks and 120 more troops to Afghanistan due to the lessons learned about the Taliban's conventional combat posture in Operation Medusa as opposed to its more traditional hit and run tactics. Smith's coverage concluded with a story on the success of Medusa in which he interviewed Asadullah Khalid, the Governor of Kandahar province and another story quoting a Taliban member who saw his comrades shredded in battle, but who vowed to fight on.

The Toronto Star

The Star carried thirty-three news stories related to Afghanistan, but only eight of those were datelined from that country, five of which were written by the Canadian Press's Les Perreaux. His most prominent pieces in The Star involved the early incidents in which four soldiers died in combat and one was killed by a U.S. strafing accident and dozens were injured. Much of the news was follow-up, reporting on the caskets returning home, the funerals, and the deceased soldiers' grieving families. In a report on September 11, Prime Minister Stephen Harper linked the mission in Afghanistan to 9/11. Three analysis pieces were written, the strongest of which argued counterfactually that, if 9/11 had never happened, no one would care about Afghanistan. Eight opinion pieces were written; the strongest two linked the Canadian combat mission to the American mission in Iraq and Prime Minister Harper following U.S. President George Bush's script. Editorially, after five soldiers were killed, the newspaper called on the prime minister to define success in Afghanistan and, in a second, said Canada's role in Afghanistan was justified and condemned the New Democratic Party for vote-pandering on the back of the Canadian deaths. There was no wrap-up story saying Operation Medusa had been a success.

The Vancouver Sun

The Sun carried twenty-one news stories and three editorials during the period of Operation Medusa. Only five of the news stories identified as coming from CanWest News Services were datelined Afghanistan. The balance originated in Vancouver and Ottawa. The most prominent news stories reported the deaths of four Canadians killed in early combat and one accidently killed in a U.S. strafing while dozens of others were injured. Most of the stories followed up on the deaths with stories originating in Canada and the New Democratic Party's demands for Canada to pull out of Afghanistan. Prime Minister Stephen Harper linked the mission in Afghanistan to 9/11 in a September 11 follow-up. The newspaper wrapped up its Medusa coverage with the Calgary Herald's Renata D'Aliesio's story on Medusa's success in which she quoted Brigadier General David Fraser, the Canadian NATO commander in southern Afghanistan. Editorially, the newspaper criticized the New Democratic Party's stand on Afghanistan and called for NATO's European members to commit more troops to the Afghan mission.

Winnipeg Free Press

The Free Press carried sixteen news stories on Afghanistan, all of which were written by either CanWest News Service or Canadian Press writers. The majority of the stories reported or followed up on the combat deaths of four Canadian soldiers early in Operation Medusa and a friendly-fire incident in which one Canadian was killed and dozens of others wounded when a U.S.

warplane accidently strafed them. On September 11, Prime Minster Stephen Harper was reported linking 9/11 to the Afghan mission. The newspaper's coverage concluded with a Canadian Press/Associated Press story on the success of Medusa in which Asadullah Khalid, the Governor of Kandahar province, was interviewed. A second story on the same day was a CanWest news service report that the Canadian deaths in Afghanistan were far greater than Americans, quoting the left-wing Centre for Policy Alternatives.

Discussion and Conclusions

Comparing case studies of English-language news media reports from the First World War, the Second World War, Korea, the 1991 Persian Gulf War, the 1999 Kosovo Air War, and the war against insurgents in Afghanistan is interesting. However, it must be noted that case study research is always limited in what it can conclude. One battle does not a war make, and one may win a battle but still lose the war. No conclusions can be extrapolated to French Canadian news media, or radio, or television. Still, the comparisons show that the low point in Canadian war journalism must surely be Max Aitken's reporting from the First World War in which he refused to go to the front lines and, instead, chose to pen upbeat reports about battles, including the disaster at St. Eloi's craters.

One of the most stirring accounts of Canadians in battle must certainly be Ross Munro's account of the Canadian assault on Dieppe during the Second World War. Unfortunately, he neglected to report that Canadians were slaughtered on the beaches. Brave as he was for being there in the first place and returning to the beaches in a landing craft, it would have helped if he had told the catastrophic truth about it. Later, it eventually came out anyway, no thanks to Munro. Even though there was official government-mandated censorship during the First and Second World Wars, there was no real need to censor either Aitken or Munro; they censored themselves.

That Bill Boss lived through the Battle of Kap'yong during the Korean War and was able to report on it is astonishing. His report of that battle is one of the greatest journalism stories of all time and he is the one who should be lionized in Canadian journalism history, not Munro. What is enlightening about Boss's reports is that the newspapers that ran them indicated they were censored so he could not report soldiers' names, hometown, or the battle's location. The newspapers found a way around the location censorship by indicating that it was likely imposed by the military and not the government. It is passing strange that soldiers' names could not be used. Names give life to words on a page and it is unlikely in the days when television was still in its infancy that identified soldiers could face retribution for their actions.

The 1991 Persian Gulf War must be seen as the beginning of institution-alizing Canadian military restrictions and censorship on the news media with the development of the first embedding agreement. The newspapers of the day were correct to see it for what it was: censorship. It would be just the tip of the iceberg.

The Canadian news media coverage of the 1999 Kosovo Air War scrapes near the bottom of the barrel. Military commanders did not give journalists access to their men and women out of mythical operational security concerns emanating from the 1991 Persian Gulf War. In doing so, they completely undermined one of the values the military in Canada's democracy is sup-posed to defend: freedom of the news media subject only to such reasonable limits in law demonstrable in a free and democratic society. That they failed to do so is reprehensible.

The Afghanistan news coverage case study shows a number of things. In the first instance, covering a war is not like reporting a train wreck in Canada. If a journalist is not there to eyewitness a battle, he or she cannot jump in a cab and catch the aftermath. The *Globe and Mail*'s Smith was the only journalist on the ground to cover the September 5 battle in Panjwaii and, thus, was the only one able to report on it. This is not a condemnation of the other journalists risking their lives covering Operation Medusa; they just were not in the neighbourhood. A second thing that the Medusa case study shows is that it was a one-of-a-kind battle. It is not reasonable to expect the kind of coverage Bill Boss delivered during the pitched battle at Kap'yong or Smith delivered in Panjwaii every day. It was not possible during the Korean War and it is even less possible in the war against insurgents in Afghanistan. They are not the same kind of wars, again demonstrating the limitations of case study research and its conclusions.

A third thing, however, that the Medusa news media case study points toward is the homogeneity of the Canadian news media. Even across com-petitors in different cities, the news media coverage was remarkably similar. Having said that, a fourth thing it points toward is that, while there is generic homogeneity, editors also have wide latitude to pick and chose which repor-ter's stories they use. Clearly, with the *Calgary Herald*'s Renata D'Aliesio embed-ded, they used her material the most. Other CanWest newspapers did not.

Fifth, the Medusa case shows the tremendous agenda-setting power of the prime minister. When Stephen Harper linked 9/11 to Canada's role in Afghanistan on September 11, 2006, his argument was dutifully reported. But, in one of the most heated battles of the conflict, with Canadians dying in record numbers, the prime minister spoke only once.

The sixth thing the Medusa case study confirms is the truism that, "if it bleeds, it leads." The stories that appeared about Medusa's success at the time were overshadowed, if not overwhelmed, by the sheer volume of reporting on the four soldiers killed on the first day of battle, the pictures of ramp ceremonies, the follow-ups on the coffins' return to Canada and the funerals. Obviously, situations can change over time, but it could have been reported at the time that the four did not die in vain.

From the qualitative newspaper evidence and interviews, there can be little doubt that the Canadian news media in Afghanistan is restricted in its coverage of the mission by the ground rules agreement and pressure from commanders and public affairs officers. It would be incorrect, however, to say that the restrictions placed on the media by the embedding agreement are uniform. They seem to vary from commander to commander, from public affairs officer to public affairs officer, and from situation to situation. The one thing that can be said, however, is that, should the need arise, the embedding agreement can be dusted off at any time to serve "operational security" as the military sees fit. It takes a courageous journalist, indeed, to stand up to the military in such situations.

The evidence firmly establishes the news media coverage of Afghanistan on a historical continuum where Bill Boss's reporting of Kap'yong stands out like a healthy thumb on a sore hand. The news media embedding program in Afghanistan is, at best, imperfect and, at worst, the lesser of two evils. While arguments have been made that reporters must find ways to report on Canada's role independently, it is difficult to conceive how such can be done safely. The one reporter who tried it, the *Globe and Mail*'s Graeme Smith, was targeted by gunmen who sacked his office compound and beat up his cook. It is argued that the public's right to know is not worth the life of one soldier. It can also be argued that the public's right to know is not worth the life of one journalist. That Smith had the courage to routinely unembed himself and travel into some of the most dangerous places in the world at great risk to his own personal well-being is commendable, to say the very least.

Smith is also correct in saying that the Canadian news media industry is failing Canadians badly during Canada's single largest foreign policy commitment since the Korean War. At time of writing, 132 soldiers and one diplomat had lost their lives in Afghanistan. Yet, only one reporter, Smith, was permanently assigned to Afghanistan. This is appalling. At the same time, it is difficult to argue that Canadian journalists should be compelled to live and work permanently in Afghanistan as Smith did.

The alternatives that have arisen in absence of such a commitment are also commendable. It is encouraging that a handful of senior journalists return time and again for their news outlets and news services. They know the grave peril that awaits them in Afghanistan, unlike first-timers who know not what they ask for when they agree to embed in Afghanistan.

That hundreds have agreed to embed is encouraging because that means that hundreds of journalists have been exposed to the Canadian Forces who had not been before. What is less encouraging is that, once back in Canada, few see the need to ever report on the military again. It is as if having an Afghan visa in their passport is a rite of passage. Unlike the military, journalists have no collective memory, no body of wisdom that can be systematically passed along, not from just one journalist to the next, but from one generation to another. As imperfect as the embedding agreement is, Canadians are also not well served by most of the news media that is not well positioned to challenge restrictions the military imposes. They deserve much better.

There is even worse news: the military tried to restrict an academic who dared to research precisely that issue. Canadians deserve much better from their military on that front, as well.

Bob Bergen, Ph.D.

Dr. Bob Bergen is an adjunct assistant professor in the University of Calgary's Centre for Military and Strategic Studies and a Fellow of the Canadian Defence & Foreign Affairs Institute. He holds a Bachelor of Arts degree in English Literature from Brock University in St. Catharines, Ontario; a Master of Communications Studies degree from the U of C; and a Ph.D. in Strategic Studies from the U of C's Center for Military and Strategic Studies.

Bob is a former journalist who began specializing in covering the Canadian Forces in the mid-1970s at The Albertan where his work revealing Canadian soldiers in Calgary were on provincial welfare roles prompted federal changes to the Forces housing policies and won The Albertan a Governor-General's citation for Meritorious Public Service in Canadian Journalism in 1979. He joined The Albertan's Editorial Board in 1979 and left for the Calgary Herald in 1980 where he also sat on the Editorial Board in 1982-1983. He wrote on the federal goverenment during the eras of Prime Ministers Pierre Trudeau, Joe Clark and Brian Mulroney.

His coverage of the Forces included assignments on United Nations and North Atlantic Treaty Organization operations in the Middle East (1977), Cyprus (1978), Cold War Europe (1978) and in Croatia and Bosnia (1994). He also attended the National Security Studies Course at National Defence College (March –April, 1992)

He began his Ph.D. studies on a part-time basis in May 1999 and left the Calgary Herald in July 2000 after 20 years to pursue those studies full-time. In 2001-2002, he was the Media Fellow with the Sheldon Chumir Foundation for Ethics in Leadership. His doctoral dissertation researched the Canadian Forces management of the Canadian news media in Ottawa and in Aviano, Italy, during the 1999 Kosovo air war. He was awarded his Ph.D. in 2005.

In December 2007, Dr. Bergen participated in a fact finding trip to North Atlantic Treaty Organization Headquarters in Brussels, Belgium; NATO headquarters in Kabul and ISAF operations in Kandahar, Afghanistan, that was jointly organized by NATO and the Department of National Defence for Security and Defence Forum academics.

Appendix One

Attachment 3

ADM(PA)J5PA Instruction 0301
12 November 2003

List of releasable and non-releasable information for Embedded Media.

Non-releasable information

1. Unless specifically approved by the Commander Task Force or designated officer, the following categories of information are not releasable since their publication or broadcast could jeopardize operations and endanger lives.

    a.   Specific information on troop strength, equipment or critical supplies (e.g. artillery, radars, trucks, water, etc.).

    b.   Specific number of aircraft in units below wing level, or identification of mission aircraft points of origin, other than land or carrier based. Number and type of aircraft may be described in very general terms such as "large flight," "small flight," "many," "few," "fighters," "fixed wing," etc.

    c.   Units in the Area of Operation, unless specifically authorized by a release authority.

    d.   Information regarding future operations, current operations, postponed or cancelled operations, or information regarding security precautions at military installations or encampments.

    e.   Photography that would show level of security at military installations or encampments, especially aerial and satellite photography which would reveal the name of specific location of military units or installations.

    f.   Rules of Engagement.

    g.   Name of military installations or specific geographic locations of military units in the area of responsibility.

    h.   Information on intelligence collection activities including targets, methods of attack and results.

    j.   Extra precaution in reporting will be required at the start of an operation to maximize operational surprise. Therefore, broadcasts from airfields by embedded media members are prohibited until authorized by the unit commander.

k. During an operation, specific information on friendly fire force troop movements, tactical deployments; and dispositions that would jeopardize operational security or lives. Information on on-going engagements will not be released unless authorized by the on-scene commander.

m. Information on postponed or cancelled operations

n. Information on missing or downed aircraft while search and rescue and recovery operations are being planned and executed.

p. Information on special operations units.

q. Information on effectiveness of enemy electronic warfare.

r. Information on effectiveness of enemy camouflage, deception, targeting, direct and indirect fire, intelligence collection or security measures.

s. No photographs or other visual media showing a detained person's recognizable face, nametag or other identifying feature or item may be taken.

t. Information regarding force protection measures at military installations of encampments, except those that are visible or readily apparent.

u. No still or video of deployed special operations forces.

v. Any other information that may be restricted from time to time by the Commander Canadian Forces Task Force due to operational requirements.

Releasable Information

2. The following categories of information are releasable.

a. Arrival of military units in the area of operation when officially announced. Mode of travel (sea or air), dates of departure, and home station.

b. Approximate friendly force strength figures.

c. Non-sensitive, unclassified information regarding air and ground past operations.

d. Size of friendly force participating in an action or operation may be disclosed using general terms such as "multi-unit." Specific force or unit identification may be released when authorized by the Commander Canadian Forces Task Force or his designate.

e. Generic description of origin of air operations, such as "land-based."

f. Date, time or location of completed military missions and actions as well as mission results.

g. Type of ordnance expended in general terms.

h. Number of aerial combat or reconnaissance missions or sorties flown in the Area of Operation.

j. Type of forces involved (e.g. air defence, infantry, amour) with exception of Special Forces.

k. Weather and climate conditions.

Notes

1   Canada. Department of National Defence. DAOD 2008-4. Public Affairs, Military Doctrine and Canadian Forces Operations. From the Internet: http://admfincs.forces/subjects/daod/2008/4_e.asp [Accessed June 23, 2005].

2   Omar L. Akkad, "Detainee file was overseen by 'Tiger Team': added scrutiny caused many delays." *The Globe and Mail*, January 3, 2008, A1.

3   Ibid.

4   Ibid.

5   Canada: Canadian Expeditionary Force, ADM (PA) Instruction 0601, April, 2006.

6   Canada: Canadian Expeditionary Force. 1350-1 (CEFCOM PA) 21 April 2006. Annex A 1350-1 (CEFCOM PA) March 2006. The Media Embedding program documents currently in use at time of writing has one addition to that clause "when directed." The current documents are undated.

7   Ibid., ADM (PA) Instruction 0601, April, 2006.

8   Conrad Russell, *Academic Freedom* (Florence: Routledge, 1993), 3. http://site.ebrary.com/lib/ucalgary/Doc?id=2003065&ppg=15

9   W.H. Kesterton, *A History of Journalism in Canada* (Toronto: McClelland & Stewart, 1967), 246.

10 Jeffrey A. Keshen, *Propaganda and Censorship during Canada's Great War* (Edmonton: University of Alberta Press, 1996), xiii.

11 Ibid., 12–13.

12 Max Aitken, quoted in ibid. Keshen, *Propaganda and Censorship during Canada's Great War*, 31–32.

13 "Galantry of the Canadians. Many daring deeds by Ontario soldiers: Thrilling Narratives of Bravery and Perseverance in Fighting of the 18th, 19th, 20th and 21st Battalions told Hold Line in Front of St. Eloi." *The Globe*, April 24, 1916, 1.

14 Colonel G.W.L. Nicholson, *Canadian Expeditionary Force 1914–1919* (Ottawa: Queen's Printer, 1962), 145.

15 Keshen, *Propaganda and Censorship during Canada's Great War*, 32.

16 Humboldt Wolfe, "Over the Fire." in *The Uncelestial City* (New York: A. A. Knopf, 1930), 37.

17 Kesterton, *A History of Journalism in Canada*, 247.

18 Ibid., 248.

19 David J. Bercuson, *Maple Leaf against the Axis: Canada's Second World War* (Toronto: Stoddart, 1995), 61.

20 Ross Munro, *Gauntlet to Overlord: The Story of the Canadian Army* (Toronto: Macmillan, 1946), 297.

21 Phillip Knightley, *The First Casualty* (New York: Harcourt Brace Jovanovich, 1975), 318; Terence Robertson, *Shame and the Glory: Dieppe* (McClelland & Stewart, 1962), 395.

22 Terence Robertson, *Dieppe: Shame and the Glory* (Little, Brown and Co., 1962), 395.

23 A.E. Powley, *Broadcast from the Front: Canadian Radio Overseas in the Second World War* (Toronto: A.M. Hakkert, 1975), 11.

24 Ibid., 30.

25 Robertson, *Dieppe*, 156.

26 Wallace Reyburn, "Street Fighting in Dieppe," *Life* (Chicago: Time Inc., August 31, 1942), 35–38.

27 Powley, *Broadcast from the Front*, 32–33.

28 Ibid., 329.

29 Ibid., 329–30.

30 Ibid., 334.

31 Ibid., 326.

32 "Raid, Not an Invasion, Radio Warns French," *Globe and Mail*, August 19, 1942.

33 "Canadians in Commando Raid," *Calgary Herald*, August 19, 1942.

34 Louis F. Keemle, "Raid Sets Pattern for Invasion," *Calgary Herald*, August 19, 1942.

35 Ibid.

36 Ross Munro, "I saw Canadian Heroes Die at Dieppe," *Vancouver Sun*, August 21, 1942.

37 "Ross Munro Story Called Masterpiece," *Vancouver Sun*, August 21, 1942.

38 "War stories given praise," *Globe and Mail*, August 22, 1942.

39 Munro, *Gauntlet to Overlord*, 337.

40 Ibid., 309–310.

41 Ibid., 314.

42 Ibid., 316.

43 Ibid., 337.

44 Ibid., 339.

45 Knightly, *The First Casualty*, 319.

46 Daniel C. Hallin, *The "Uncensored War": The Media and Vietnam* (Berkeley: University of California Press, 1986); Todd Gitlin, *The Whole World is Watching: Mass Media in the Making and Unmaking of the New Left* (Berkeley: University of California Press, 1980); W. Lance Bennett, and David L Paletz, eds., *Taken by Storm: The Media, Public Opinion, and U.S. Foreign Policy in the Gulf War* (Chicago: University of Chicago Press, 1994); Robert A. Hackett, *News and Dissent: the Press and the Politics of Peace in Canada* (Norwood: Ablex, 1991).

47 Knightley, *The First Casualty*, 319.

48 David J. Bercuson, *Blood on the Hills: The Canadian Army in the Korean War* (Toronto: University of Toronto Press, 1999), 106–111.

49 Olen Clements, "Mongol Hordes Spearhead Drive: Reds Rip Gaping Hole in UN Line, Pour South" *Globe and Mail*, April 24, 1951, 1; "500,000 Reds Smash Allied Line." *Vancouver Sun*, April 24, 1951; "Allies Unable to Hold Line, 500,000 Reds Launch Attack." *Calgary Herald*, April 24, 1951, 1; "Chinese Smash Open Allied Line," *The Albertan*, April 24, 1951, 1. "Waves of Red Troops Force Allies Back Along

Central Front," *Halifax Chronicle-Herald*, 1.

50   Ibid.

51   "Reds Surge towards Seoul," *Vancouver Sun*, April 26, 1951, 1.

52   Bill Boss, "Outflanked, encircle Pats won't Quit, Beat Back Reds, Hurl Rifles like spears," *Toronto Daily Star*, April 26, 1951, 1.

53   Ibid.

54   Bill Boss, "Communists Fail to Budge Troops," *The Albertan*, April 26, 1951, 1; William Boss, "Flanks, Rear Cleared, Enemy Held in Front," *Globe and Mail*, April 26, 1951, 1.

55   Bill Boss, "Cut Off, Encircled in Hills, Pats Hold Steady as Rocks: Flanks, Rear Relieved, Enemy Held in Front." *Globe and Mail*, April 26, 1951, 1; Bill Boss, "Communists Fail to Budge Troops," *The Albertan*, April 26, 1951, 1.

56   "Chinese Forcing Retreat," *Halifax Chronicle-Herald*, April 26, 1951, 1.

57   For an in-depth examination of the Canadian Forces public affairs plan and analysis of its effects, see: Robert W. Bergen, *Balkan Rats and Balkan Bats: The Art of Managing Canada's News Media during the Kosovo Air War*. 2005. A doctoral thesis at the University of Calgary pending publication by UBC Press.

58   Ibid.

59   Canada. Department of National Defence. After Action Report Operation Friction: Director General Public Affairs. 24 July 1991. Obtained under *Access to Information Act* request A-2003-00394.

60   National Defence. Department of National Defence. Operation Friction: Canadian Forces Operations in the Persian Gulf Communications Plan. 9 November 90. Obtained under *Access to Information Act* request A-2003-00394.

61   Ibid. Please note that in the original Canadian Forces documents, there were no "i" or "o" letters.

62   Robert W. Bergen, *Balkan Rats and Balkan Bats*, 78.

63   Canada. National Defence. After Action Report: Gulf War Public Affairs. Director General Public Affairs. 23 April 1991. Obtained under the Access to Information Act: file number A-2003-00394.

64   Philip M. Taylor, "War and the Media," unpublished paper delivered at a military-media relations conference at Royal Military Academy at Sandhurst in 1995, p. 10 of 13. From the Internet: http://www.leeds.ac.uk/ics/arts-pt2.htm [Accessed August 10, 2004].

65   Philip M. Taylor, "War and the Media," 11.

66   Ibid.

67   Robert W. Bergen, *Balkan Rats and Balkan Bats*, 342.

68   Ibid., 285.

69   Ibid., 343.

70   Transcript briefing by DCDS – Media Q in (1 June 99). From the Internet: http://dgpa-dgpa.mil.ca/Transcr/1999Jun/99060105.htm [Accessed July 16, 2003] Obtained from National Defence Public Affairs Office – Calgary.

71   Ibid.

72   Transcript briefing by DCDS – Media Q in (2 June 99). From the Internet: http://dgpa-dgpa.mil.ca/Transcr/1999Jun/99060209.htm [Accessed July 16, 2003] Obtained from National Defence Public Affairs Office – Calgary.

73   Ibid.

74   For a full examination of Canadian Forces management of the Canadian news media coverage of the Kosovo air war and its results, see Robert W. Bergen, *Balkan Rats and Balkan Bats*, 258–394.

75   Ibid., 368.

76   Canada. National Defence Headquarters. Defence Ethics Program. "Ethics and Operations Project: Project Report." 9 March 2000, 8. From the Internet: http://www.dnd.ca/ethics/pages/kdocs_e.htm [Accessed September 25, 2003].

77   Canada. Department of National Defence. *Public Affairs Handbook* (Ottawa: Director General Public Affairs, 1999).

78   *The Canadian Press Stylebook*, 14th ed. (Toronto: Canadian Press, 2006), 253–55.

79   Major J. Janzen, "OP Athena ROTO 0-Embedded Media," *Canadian Army Journal* 7, nos. 3-4 (Fall/Winter 2004): 43–51.

80   Ibid., 43–44.

81   Ibid., 44.

82   Ibid., 45.

83   Ibid., 46.

84   Ibid., 47–48.

85   Canada. Canadian Forces (ADM(PA/ J5PA Instruction 0301). 12 November 2003.

86   Ibid.

87   Ibid.

88   Ibid.

89   Ibid.

90   Stephen Thorne, "The Enemy Within: Generals Deal Blow to Embed Program," *Canadian War Correspondents Association Newsletter*, Fall 2004.

91   Ibid.

92   Ibid.

93   Ibid.

94   Ibid.

95   *The Province* (Vancouver) reported that the village was Shinkay, about 70 km north of Kandahar. Susan Lazaruk, "B.C. soldier critical after Afghan at-tack," *The Province*, March 5, 2008. From the Internet http:www.missing-people.net/trevor_greene_Vancouver.htm [Accessed November 28, 2008]. *Globe and Mail* identified only the village, Shinkay, and not its location. Ha, Tu Thanh. "Military rethinks Afghan tactics," *Globe and Mail*, March 6, 2006, A1.

96   Mitch Potter, "Axe Attack," *Toronto Star*, March 5, 2006, A1, A10–11.

97   Ibid.

98   Les Perreaux, "Canadian soldier hurt in axe attack," *Chronicle-Herald*, March 5, 2006, A1; Les Perreaux, "Soldier wounded in axe attack," *Winnipeg Free Press*, March 5, 2006, A1; Chris Wattie, "B.C. soldier badly hurt in brutal at-tack," *Times Colonist* (Victoria), March 5, 2006, A1; Chris Wattie, "Axe fells Canadian soldier," *Edmonton Journal*, March 5, 2006, A1; Chris Wattie, "Canadian soldier ambushed with axe: Quiet meeting with elders erupts in chaos," *Calgary Herald*, March 5, 2006, A3; Chris Wattie, "Canadian Soldiers Ambushed," *The Gazette* (Montreal), March 5, 2006, A1; Tu Thann Ha, "Military rethinks tactics," *The Globe and Mail*, March 6, 2006, A1; Chris Wattie and Carly Weeks, "Crash claims second soldier," *National Post* (Toronto), March 6, 2006, A1; Chris Wattie and Carly Weeks, "Layton urges Afghan debate," *The Windsor Star*, March 6, 2006, A1; Chris Wattie, "Soldier 'completely vulnerable' in axe attack," *Star Phoenix* (Saskatchewan), March 6, 2006, D8.

99   Captain (N) Chris Henderson, "Reporting Live from Kanadar," *Canadian Military Journal* (Summer 2006): 85–88.

100   "Access comes with risks," *The Toronto Star*, April 8, 2006, F06.

101   Ibid.

102   Christie Blatchford, "A far more insidi-ous form of 'embedding,'" *The Globe and Mail*, April 8, 2006, A15.

103 http://www.unicef.org/infobycountry/ afghanistan_statistics.html

104 Christie Blatchford, "A far more insidious form of 'embedding,'" *The Globe and Mail*. As late as March 2008, *Globe and Mail* had taken to incorporating the term "researcher" in a story on why the Taliban embrace suicide bombings and in which a fixer was the information gatherer. Graeme Smith's front-page story, "Why the Taliban now embrace the concept of suicide bombing," on March 28, was highly informative and upfront about who gathered the raw information, but there will always be a "but" associated with such stories.

105 Jeff Esau, "Canadian military yanks embedded journalists after complaints from allies," *Canadian Press*, Toronto, December 30, 2006. Nothing was written about the incident by Blatchford in the entire month of January 2007, following.

106 Geoffrey York, "Dispatches from an embedded life," *The Globe and Mail*, June 3, 2006, F2.

107 Ibid.

108 Ibid.

109 Steven Chase, "PM's office sought 'a positive spin' from reporters," *The Globe and Mail*, June 4, 2008, A5.

110 Bob Bergen, "Disarming the Media: At Wainwright, troops are trained to confront an unpredictable force: the people who bring us the news," *Alberta Views* (April 2007): 40–43.

111 Ibid.

112 Ibid.

113 Canada. Canadian Forces Commander, Canadian Expeditionary Force Command. 1350-1 (CEFCOM PA, February 2007. OP ATHENA – MEDIA EMBED PROGRAM (MEP) INSTRUCTIONS. Annex A. 1350-1 9CEFCOM PA) February 2007, A-3/3.

114 Graham Thomson, "Embedded: an uneasy truce," *Edmonton Journal*, April 15, 2007, D6-7.

115 Ibid.

116 Ibid.

117 Sharon Hobson, "The Information Gap: Why the Canadian Public Doesn't Know More About its Military" (Calgary: Canadian Defence &Foreign Affairs Institute, June 2007), 13.

118 Ibid., 14.

119 Ibid.

120 Richard Latendress, "Reporting, military style," *Calgary Sun*, September 11, 2007, 15.

121 Jeff Heirich, "Quebec's support for war seems in freefall after latest casualties," *Calgary Herald*, August 24, 2007, A4.

122 Ibid.

123 Ibid.

124 "Canadian journalists to wear ID tags," *Prince George Citizen*, August 28, 2007, 1.

125 Canada. Department of National Defence. DAOD 2008-4. Public Affairs, Military Doctrine and Canadian Forces Operations. From the Internet: http://admfincs.forces.gc.ca/admfincs/ subjects/daod/2008/4_e.asp [Accessed June 23, 2005].

126 Due to changes in titles, the 2005 website document makes the assistant deputy minister for public affairs (ADM [PA]) responsible for the development of a national public affairs plan, but, in 1999, the person responsible for the plan was the director general public affairs (DGPA).

127 Ibid.

128 Ibid.

129 Brigadier· General Peter Atkinson, ADM(PA) Transcript. "Government Officials hold technical briefing to provide an update on Canada's activities in Afghanistan," *Media Q*, 14 February

2008. Obtained from National Defence Public Affairs Office, Prairies and NWT, February 15, 2008.

130 Major Jay Janzen, interview with author, January 16, 2008.

131 Ibid.

132 Confidential interview with author, May, 2007.

133 Major Jay Janzen, interview with author, January 16, 2008.

134 Ibid.

135 Ibid.

136 Ibid.

137 Captain Joanne Blais, interview with author, Camp Nathan Smith, Kandahar, Afghanistan, December 17, 2007.

138 Ibid.

139 Ibid.

140 Timothea Gibb, interview with author, Camp Nathan Smith. Kandahar, Afghanistan, December 17, 2007.

141 Bill Graveland, interview with author, January 16, 2008.

142 Ibid.

143 Graeme Smith, interview with author, March 12, 2008.

144 Ibid.

145 Ibid.

146 Ibid.

147 Ibid.

148 Ibid.

149 Graveland has since returned to Afghanistan a third time.

150 Renata D'Aliesio, interview with author, March 26, 2008

151 "Operation Medusa Foiled Taliban Plans, NATO Commander Says," American Government – U.S. Department of State. From the Internet: http:www.america.gov/st/ washfile-enlgish/2006/September/20

060920172756adynned0.4... [Accessed December 2, 2008].

152 Renata D'Aliesio, interview with author.

153 Ibid.

154 Ibid.

155 Ibid.

156 "Operation Medusa Foiled Taliban Plans, NATO Commander Says," American Government – U.S. Department of State. From the Internet: http:www.america.gov/st/ washfile-enlgish/2006/September/20 060920172756adynned0.4... [Accessed December 2, 2008]

ORDER FORM

To order a copy of *Calgary Papers in Military and Strategic Studies* or an *Occasional Paper*, please mail this form with your cheque (made out to the Centre for Military and Strategic Studies) to the address below. Send only your mailing address if you represent a library, research centre or government agency, as the cost is waived for those institutions. We will then add you to our regular mailing list to receive this and future issues. (US and International orders should send Canadian or US fund, please.)

Calgary Papers in Military and Strategic Studies

VOLUME AND TITLE	PRICE	# OF COPIES	SUBTOTAL	TOTAL
Vol. 1, 2007 - Paperback - *Canada in Kandahar*	$15			
Vol. 1, 2007 - Hardcover - *Canada in Kandahar*	$20			
Vol. 2, 2007 - Paperback - *Canadian Defence Policy*	$15			
Vol. 1, 2008 - Paperback - *Strategic Studies*	$15			
Vol. 2, 2008 - Hardcover - *Military Studies and History*	$20			
Vol. 3, 2008 - Hardcover - *Civil-Military Coordination: Challenges and Opportunities in Afghanistan and Beyond*	$20			
OCCASIONAL PAPERS				
No. 1, 2008 - *Lock, Stock, and Icebergs? Defining Canadian Sovereignty from Mackenzie King to Stephen Harper*	$7.50			
No. 2, 2008 - *Equipment Procurement in Canada and the Civil-Military Relationship: Past and Present*	$7.50			
No. 3, 2009 - *Censorship: the Canadian News Media and Afghanistan: A Historical Comparison with Case Studies*	$7.50			

NAME: **EMAIL** (OPTIONAL)**:**

MAILING ADDRESS:

MAIL TO: The Centre for Military and Strategic Studies, MacKimmie Library Tower 701,
University of Calgary, 2500 University Drive NW, Calgary, Alberta T2N 1N4
Fax: 403-282-0594   Telephone: 403-220-4038